Look for more books in the Wilson Family Series:

by Doug Wilson:

Reforming Marriage

Her Hand in Marriage

Standing on the Promises:
A Handbook on Biblical Childrearing

Federal Husband

Future Men

by Nancy Wilson:

Fruit of Her Hands:
Respect and the Christian Woman

Praise Her in the Gates:
The Calling of Christian Motherhood

Fidelity

FIDELITY

What It Means To Be a
One-Woman Man

DOUGLAS WILSON

MOSCOW, IDAHO

Douglas Wilson, *Fidelity: What It Means To Be a One-Woman Man*

© 1999 by Douglas Wilson
Published by Canon Press, P.O. Box 8741, Moscow, ID 83843
www.canonpress.org
800-488-2034

05 06 07   10 9 8 7 6 5 4

Cover design by Paige Atwood

Cover art: Frank Cadogan Cowper (1877-1958), *Vanity*, 1907, oil on panel, 54 x 37 cm, Royal Academy of Arts, London.

Printed in the United States of America.

Unless otherwise noted, Scripture quotations are taken from the King James Version of the Bible.

ISBN: 1-885767-64-1

ISBN-13: 978-1-885767-64-6
ISBN-10: 1-885767-64-1
Fidelity

Contents

Introduction

Not that this is a new development or anything, but we do live in a time when sexual fidelity is under assault. But although sexual immorality is not new in the world, certain aspects of our current situation *are* comparatively new. The novelty of our circumstance is that, driven by the forces of relativism, our culture across the board is assaulting, for the first time in millennia, the very concept of sexual fidelity.

From the very beginning, the believer has had to stand against the various temptations to sexual laxity. Because of the success of the gospel, the nations influenced by it came, over the course of centuries, to acknowledge the essential "rightness" of Christian sexual morality. This did not mean that it was consistently practiced, but it did mean that the biblical standard became a cultural norm. The word was not yet on tablets of human hearts, but at least it was inscribed on tablets of stone.

In this situation, believers have sought to live the complete standard as God teaches us in His Word. But we are rapidly reverting to the *status quo ante;* we are quickly sliding back to paganism. Our situation is now far closer to that of the first century Corinthians, who had to deal with the sanctified brothel dedicated to Venus, than it is to the immorality of Victorian London. The prostitutes of that city conducted a thriving trade among nominal Christians who knew their hypocrisy. But we are no longer good enough to be hypocrites.

Chastity was a novelty introduced to the Gentile

nations as a result of the preaching of the gospel. Other virtues had been acknowledged by the pagans, and the Christian faith provided the grace and strength to live up to the standard that had always been acknowledged and admired. But biblical chastity was a cultural offense and took more than a little getting used to. Because the gospel transforms cultures as well as lives, the power of the gospel brought to our peoples what we might call sexual civilization.

But because of the general doctrinal apostasy of evangelical churches over the last century and a half, we find that our influence as salt and light is no longer what it was. A century ago an immoral man would avoid the Christians with shame in his face. Today, the promiscuous just stare at us blankly. We must return to our prior understanding of the Word of God and rebuild our understanding of sexual morality. But in far too many instances the world is having a much greater influence on the church than *vice versa*.

This book is not the place to develop the doctrinal issues, which has been capably done by others elsewhere. But with that doctrinal basis assumed, the structure of Christian sexual morality must be restored and reformed.

In the pastoral epistles, the apostle Paul sets down a requirement that each Christian elder be a "one-woman man"—the husband of one woman. This pattern is required of all Christian leaders so that they can exhibit the definition of Christian marriage to all the followers of Christ. The disciples, in turn, are to imitate what they see. The Bible requires the elders of the church to be *devoted to one woman*, and it requires the people of God to watch all this closely, among other things, and imitate it—"Remember them which have the rule over you, who have spoken unto you the word of God: whose faith follow, considering the end of their conversation" (Heb. 13:7).

So what does it mean to be devoted to one woman? We are surrounded by a world which specializes in the various arts of inflaming lust and encouraging people, if they can't be with the one they love, to love the one they're with. In such circumstances, what are we to do? The first chapter will provide a brief defense of the straight talk approach taken throughout the book. The world does not hesitate to tempt us with messages that are not hard to understand. Unfortunately, many of the Christian responses are not nearly as clear or intelligible. The following chapters will consider in turn the various allurements which distract Christian men from their sexual responsibilties. Wading in from the shallow end of the pool, we will consider lust and pornography, then fornication, then adultery, then divorce, then prostitution, then rape, then polygamy, then sodomy, then masturbation, and finally celibacy. Because sexual temptation in each situation will be, at the root, *sexual*, this means that the various chapters will be somewhat repetitive at some points. But on a subject such as this, to write the same things is not grievous, and to the reader it is safe (Phil. 3:1).

At the same time, in writing on these things, it has been necessary (on some subjects) to go out on a limb. I am certainly aware that there is room for disagreement in what has been argued at certain places, but I have ventured into some controversial areas regardless. This is because too often pastoral advice on certain delicate issues has been developed by pastors in isolation—we have not been talking about these things with one another, or when we *have* talked about them, we have been simply recycling the work of unbelieving sexual therapists for Christian consumption. We have to do better than this, and so exegetical discussion on practices like masturbation and oral sex should at the very least be initiated.

Having considered the particular temptations which attend the subject matter of each chapter, we will conclude with the antidote to all sexual disease, which is the godly honoring of the marriage bed: "Marriage is honourable in all, and the bed undefiled: but whoremongers and adulterers God will judge" (Heb. 13:4). And we will come to understand that, biblically, the spiritual solution to sexual temptation can be pretty basic and earthy.

CHAPTER ONE

A Blunt Instrument

This book was written for men and their sons. I suggest that wives read this only when their husbands give it to them, and not the other way around. The introduction mentioned the issue of "straight talk"—and this means, in part, a rejection of euphemism. Some of what is said here may be offensive to some Christian women, but the point is certainly not to give offense. The point is to provide biblically specific and pointed help to Christian males.

At the same time, although I want to speak plainly enough so that what is said is a genuine help, I also want to avoid any apparent violation of Paul's injunction:

> But fornication, and all uncleanness, or covetousness, let it not be once named among you, as becometh saints; neither filthiness, nor foolish talking, nor jesting, which are not convenient: but rather giving of thanks. For this ye know, that no whoremonger, nor unclean person, nor covetous man, who is an idolater, hath any inheritance in the kingdom of Christ and of God. (Eph. 5:3–5)

Clearly Paul does not mean that such sins should not be mentioned or described—*he* mentions them here. He is saying that such things ought not to be named in our presence in any way which tolerates or gives countenance to them. We live at a time when the world does not hesitate to teach on sexual behavior. Broad evangelical churches usually mimic the world's teaching with a thin Christian gloss, and the more conservative churches hesitate to teach on this subject at all. The result is that such things are *done* among us, but in a false application of Paul's words, we still won't *name* them. We laugh at dirty jokes on the television shows we watch, but woe betide the poor idiot who tries to tell the same joke in the church foyer the next morning. His sin is not the joke, which half the church enjoyed in the privacy of their own homes, but rather his unwitting exposure of their dishonesty. And that "sin" is never tolerated, not even in times of spiritual declension.

Paul is telling us that we must not tolerate disobedience, and we must not speak as though we tolerate it. If in our attack on immorality we mention our target, in no way has there been a violation of Paul's requirement.

So in addressing the question bluntly, we are not disregarding scriptural boundaries. The Bible does not give us a list of "bad words." When we sin verbally (in what is generally and inaccurately called "swearing"), the words can be put into four general categories—swearing, cursing, vulgarity, and obscenity. Because we want life to be simple, we want God to give us a list of words which He forbids and be done with it. But we see in Scripture that within *each* of these four categories there are both unlawful and lawful uses. When we take the name of the Lord in vain, we are swearing sinfully (Exod. 20:7). When we take our oaths lawfully, we swear in His name (Deut. 6:13). When we curse maliciously, we rail against the image of God in man (Jas. 3:9). When we think of false teachers as the apostle Paul does, the curse glorifies God (Gal. 1:8). When we avoid coarse and vulgar jesting (a coarseness which frequently has to do with bodily functions), we are doing nothing other than what Paul instructs (Eph. 5:4). When Isaiah rejects the self-righteousness of sinners as nothing better than a used menstrual cloth ("filthy rags"), he is being vulgar in a most holy way—in the interests of pure truth (Is. 64:6). Sometimes a vulgarity in one era is not a vulgarity in another—"So and more also do God unto the enemies of David, if I leave of all that pertain to him by the morning light any that pisseth against the wall" (1 Sam. 25:22). And in many cases, we do not learn from the example of Scripture in these areas because our translations are cleaned up, and sometimes more than just a little. The subject in this book is sex, and so I will be addressing the obscene. The word "obscene" comes from the Greek and literally means "off stage." Those things which ought not to be done at all, and those things which should not be done in public are both obscene when done in public. Some things should not be done at all, and so are obscene. Other things should be done, but not in full public view. So whenever it becomes necessary to address such things in a public fashion, it should only be done with great care and caution, and qualified beforehand in every appropriate way. And even then, it should only be done as necessary. Everything that comes out of our mouths and word processors must be useful for *edification* (Eph. 4:29).

In certain contexts, the Scripture tells us that a godly treatment of the obscene is certainly possible. Certain things which are "obscene" are fully lawful. The lovemaking of a married couple is supposed to be "offstage." But offstage does not mean "secret." A married couple is publicly known to have a sexual relationship. When Scripture addresses such things it does so with propriety and draws a veil over it. But the veil is not *entirely* opaque. For example, we learn a great deal about the propriety of sexual exuberance from the Song of Solomon. Within the context of married love, Scripture alludes positively to all kinds of conjugal activities, which we will discuss later.

On the negative side, Ezekiel rails against the adulterous idolatry of the Israelites by using sexual imagery of the most graphic sort. He uses obscenity to reveal the *real* obscenity of doing such things in defiance of God's law. A modern analogy is the practice of pro-life activists using pictures of dismembered children in their literature. Obscene? Yes, but the point is to expose the real obscenity, which is the *practice* of dismembering them.

Ezekiel was more concerned about the obscenity he was exposing than the obscenity he was using: "Again the word of the LORD came unto me, saying, Son of man, *cause* Jerusalem to *know* her *abominations*, and say, Thus says the Lord GOD to Jerusalem" (Ezek. 16:1–3). Ezekiel was not some naughty child behind the barn, tee-heeing over his use of naughty language. He was filled with hatred for the obscenity being *committed*, and he was not so delicate that he refused to name what he was attacking. Phineas certainly observed a man and a woman copulating, but he was not doing so as a voyeur. His interest was ethical; he was *taking aim*. Ezekiel was doing the same kind of thing—

> Thou hast built thy high place at every head of the way, and hast made thy beauty to be abhorred, and hast opened thy feet [*lit.*, "spread your legs wide"; the two Hebrew words are *pasaq*, meaning *open wide*, and *regel*, meaning *legs.*] to every one that passed by, and multiplied thy whoredoms. Thou hast also committed fornication with the Egyptians thy neighbours, great of flesh [he is referring here to the size of their genitals]; and hast increased thy whoredoms, to provoke me to anger. Behold, therefore I have stretched out my hand over thee, and have diminished thine ordinary food, and delivered thee unto the will of them that hate thee, the daughters of the Philistines, which are ashamed of thy lewd way. (Ezek. 16:25–27)

But Ezekiel is not content with this. He goes on a few chapters later to explain the problem even more graphically. He is being obscene, but not sinful:

> So she discovered her whoredoms, and discovered her nakedness: then my mind was alienated from her, like as my mind was alienated from her sister. Yet she multiplied her whoredoms, in calling to remembrance the days of her youth, wherein she had played the harlot in the land of Egypt. For she doted upon their paramours, whose flesh is as the flesh of asses, and whose issue is like the issue of

horses. Thus thou calledst to remembrance the lewdness of thy youth, in bruising thy teats by the Egyptians for the paps of thy youth. (Ezek. 23:18–21)

Put into modern English, the Israelites are condemned because they lusted for those who were endowed with a penis like a donkey, who ejaculated like horses, and who squeezed Israel's nipples in the days of her youth. Now, you may well say . . . is all this really necessary? I can imagine some readers saying, "You're not Ezekiel, pal."

My point is simply to show that godly obscenity exists. Certain subjects are not automatically off-limits. Of course, we are not protected by divine inspiration, as the apostles and prophets were, and so we fall short of biblical standards in many ways—and especially in an area like this, where we have so little practice and so few godly examples. However, we must become more puritanical and less Victorian—more ethical and open, and less sanctimonious and hypocritical. I recall one time in the Navy telling some sailors that they could not see past the end of their cocks—my point was an ethical one, but not really a delicate one. The Bible describes such men as unreasoning brutes. They do not understand much, and what they *do* understand, they use to destroy themselves: "But these speak evil of those things which they know not; but what they know naturally, *as brute beasts*, in those things they corrupt themselves" (Jude 10). "Dogs can hump. What else can you do?" Scientific or medical language is not suited for a prophetic rebuke.

The reason we must learn to think this way is that for the sake of our own pious traditions we have removed from circulation certain scriptural passages which are "indelicate." As a consequence, we have practically denied what God has said when He told us that *all* Scripture is the breath of God and profitable for teaching and correction and training in righteousness (2 Tim. 3:16). Thus we should not be surprised when we find ourselves ill-equipped in this particular area. This book is intended to be read in such a way that men may come to know *exactly* the nature of the temptations which face them, so that they can know exactly what they may do to resist those temptations. Too often Christians create fuzzy word pictures which generally address the problem (i.e., we all know we are talking about sex, but no one is about to raise his hand and ask about *this* or *that*). So specific teaching is still too frequently avoided. And when Christians do get specific, they are more likely to be telling us what secular sexual therapists want us to know about prolonging orgasms than to be telling us what the Bible teaches. We need to know what the Bible teaches *specifically* and apply it specifically to our own situations.

For example, Jesus tells us that to lust after a woman is tantamount to committing adultery with her. But what *is* it to lust after her? What are we talking about? The answer is that lust is in a man who imagines or sees himself to be with a woman in some sexual way and who consequently has a physiological reaction, usually manifested by an erection. He is aroused and is physiologically interested in sexual intercourse of some description. That intercourse may be with his wife (while imagining another woman), or with a woman not his wife, or with himself by means of masturbation. Or it may not lead to any sexual climax, but rather to unfulfilled sexual frustration. Lust does not come into existence at the point of sexual release. In all such cases, Jesus describes the mental state which led to this activity, or frustrated lack of activity, as "adultery." This lust is not in view if a man merely notices that a woman is pretty. It *is* in view when he begins mentally undressing her for sexual purposes.

On the subject of divorce, the Westminster Confession notes that sinful men are apt to "study arguments" in order to get away from the teaching of Scripture on divorce. It is the same with all other sexual practices. When lust is not clearly identified at the initial point of arousal, men can draw the line in all kinds of unbiblical places after they are already in the grip of lust. For example, a man might toy with a woman sexually in his mind and yet think he has not lusted because he has not had a sexual climax. Or he might think that as long as he relieves the sexual tension with his wife, it does not matter who or what got him interested. "It doesn't matter where I get my appetite," he says, "as long as I eat at home." This is nothing but grasping at technicalities. And this kind of hair-splitting mind doesn't stop there. I have known of situations where an unmarried couple thought they were not guilty of fornication because they sought oral gratification and did not technically have sexual intercourse. Oh, good. For a minute there, the pastor was worried.

By the same token, to set the line at the birth of obvious sexual interest or arousal provides relief for men with tender consciences who have thought themselves guilty of lust when all they did was notice that a woman was attractive. But these and all such distinctions, necessary to be made, cannot be explained unless we speak plainly.

CHAPTER TWO

Lust and Pornography

> For this is the will of God, even your sanctification, that ye should abstain from fornication: That every one of you should know how to possess his vessel in sanctification and honour; not in the lust of concupiscence, even as the Gentiles which know not God: That no man go beyond and defraud his brother in any matter: because that the Lord is the avenger of all such, as we also have forewarned you and testified. For God hath not called us unto uncleanness, but unto holiness. He therefore that despiseth, despiseth not man, but God, who hath also given unto us his holy Spirit. (1 Thess. 4:3–8)

The purpose of this chapter is to address Christian men and boys on some of the practical problems resulting from the pervasiveness of pornography in our culture. This pervasiveness reflects an underlying problem with lust, which must consequently be addressed first. What the Bible calls lust creates a considerable demand, and pornography is simply one of the modern market's attempts to produce something which will meet that demand. The problem is not *outside* ourselves in the x-rated videos, or in the skin magazines, or with the porn on the net, or with Suzy Q sunbathing next door. The problem is within—even within believers. This is simply another way of saying that the problem with pornography is not the pornography.

Some professing Christian men use various kinds of

porn and defend it. Others oppose porn, but use it anyway, kicking themselves every time afterwards. Others oppose it, don't use it, but really wish they could. Their "virtue" is really more a matter of cowardice than anything else. "What if someone at church found out?" So we should see immediately that the problem of lust, and the resultant problems, are not really that simple. One of the more important lessons for us to learn is that while the occasions for sin are external and "out there," the real problem is with our lusts within.

We must come to rethink the relationship between masculinity and being seduced. John Milton uses a striking phrase in *Paradise Lost*, referring to those men who were seduced by the "daughters of men." When shown the future seduction of these men, these descendents of his, Adam attempts to blame the women involved—"Man's woe holds on the same, from Woman to begin." The angel replies to the contrary: "From Man's effeminate slackness it begins."

Effeminate slackness. Many men like to flatter themselves, thinking that the ease with which they might be seduced is somehow a masculine trait. In reality it is quite the reverse. At the heart of masculinity is the possession of authority and taking of initiative; by creation design a man is intended by God to be a *head*, a head willing to sacrifice himself. But part of our word *seduction* comes from the Latin word *duco*, which means "I lead." This original meaning carries over in our use of the word *seduction*. When a man is seduced he is being led, and when a woman seduces she is leading. So when a man is seduced (whether by a living woman or a pornographic woman is immaterial) he is relinquishing and abdicating his assigned role. While he may still perform the male role in intercourse, he is no longer masculine in the relationship. He remains biologically male, but he is no longer being covenantally masculine.

The Bible uses strong phrases to illustrate the point. The mother of King Lemuel warns him bluntly about it.

She says, *"Give not thy strength unto women*, nor thy ways to that which destroyeth kings" (Prov. 31:3). A king might think himself quite a man because he has physical access to so many women. In reality, far from exhibiting the strength of a king, he is wasting away that strength. Within marriage, biblical sexual behavior strengthens a man in his masculinity. Promiscuity and pornography drain it away.

The end of any man who gives way to the immoral woman is that of an innervated weakling. Rather than growing in manhood, he discovers at the end of his life that he had really played the fool. He finds that he has given away his honor, his years, his wealth, his labors, and his health. Not much of a man is left—

> Remove thy way far from her, and come not nigh the door of her house: lest thou give thine honour unto others, and thy years unto the cruel: lest strangers be filled with thy wealth; and thy labours be in the house of a stranger; and thou mourn at the last, when thy flesh and thy body are consumed, and say, How have I hated instruction, and my heart despised reproof; and have not obeyed the voice of my teachers, nor inclined mine ear to them that instructed me! I was almost in all evil in the midst of the congregation and assembly. (Prov. 5:8–14)

But when a man lives under the blessing of God, he learns to exercise dominion. He begins this cultural dominion in his home, with his family. If he turns away from his wife, and God wants to slap him down, He may do so by means of a loose woman: "The mouth of strange women is a deep pit: he that is abhorred of the LORD shall fall therein" (Prov. 22:14). A man who has been seduced is the antithesis of a man pursuing his God-given masculine calling. Instead of learning the meaning of headship under God, he descends to the level of a dumb animal—

> For at the window of my house I looked through my casement, and beheld among the simple ones, I discerned among the youths, a young man void of understanding,

Passing through the street near her corner; and he went the way to her house, in the twilight, in the evening, in the black and dark night: and, behold, there met him a woman with the attire of an harlot, and subtil of heart. (She is loud and stubborn; her feet abide not in her house: now is she without, now in the streets, and lieth in wait at every corner.) So she caught him, and kissed him, and with an impudent face said unto him, I have peace offerings with me; this day have I payed my vows. Therefore came I forth to meet thee, diligently to seek thy face, and I have found thee. I have decked my bed with coverings of tapestry, with carved works, with fine linen of Egypt. I have perfumed my bed with myrrh, aloes, and cinnamon. Come, let us take our fill of love until the morning: let us solace ourselves with loves. For the goodman is not at home, he is gone a long journey: He hath taken a bag of money with him, and will come home at the day appointed. With her much fair speech she caused him to yield, with the flattering of her lips she forced him. He goeth after her straightway, as an ox goeth to the slaughter, or as a fool to the correction of the stocks; till a dart strike through his liver; as a bird hasteth to the snare, and knoweth not that it is for his life. (Prov. 7:6–23)

He is described as a simple man, as one devoid of understanding. The initiative in the sexual encounter is the woman's, and she entices him contrary to the law of God. He goes with her *as an ox goes to the slaughter*. He may feel like quite a man, but he is really at the end of some woman's rope. Chesterton once commented that "free love is the direct enemy of freedom. It is the most obvious of all the bribes that can be offered by slavery." A man set free by Christ does not willingly enter into such slavery; he recognizes that the "freedoms" promised by immorality can be exercised in a six-by-six prison cell. Although a man in the midst of immorality may *feel* like she is "bringing out the man in him," Milton's phrase should still come back to haunt him—effeminate slackness.

Now to understand our attraction to pornography, we

have to understand ourselves in the light of what the Bible teaches about us and our desires.

First, the biblical standard of sexual morality is not difficult to understand. The Lord Jesus makes it plain that married men are to be absolutely faithful, mentally and physically, and single men are to be absolutely chaste, mentally and physically. His words on the subject are well-known:

> Ye have heard that it was said by them of old time, Thou shalt not commit adultery: but I say unto you, that whosoever looketh on a woman to lust after her hath committed adultery with her already in his heart. (Mt. 5:27–28)

As mentioned earlier, the problem we have in meeting this standard is not outside ourselves in pornography; the problem is in our lusts. The Bible says nothing about *Penthouse*, but quite a bit about our concupiscence, without which the bookkeeper down at *Penthouse* would have trouble making payroll. When Paul tells us to mortify our members which are on the earth, he goes on to define them. These members, still present in the believer, include a desire to do sexual wrong: "Mortify therefore your members which are upon the earth; fornication, uncleanness, inordinate affection, evil concupiscence, and covetousness, which is idolatry" (Col. 3:5).

The desire which we as Christians must battle is not just a "plain vanilla," morally neutral, biological desire for sex. We are fallen creatures, and even as Christians our redemption is not yet completed. We must still deal with the fact that we will confront desires, *coming from within ourselves*, which are attractive to us by virtue of the fact that they are prohibited by God. Paul does not tell us to restrain our sexual desires because, if we don't watch it, they *could* be put to a wrong use. These members of ours on the earth are not morally neutral; they must be mortified—put to death. Paul here uses the aorist imperative which indicates a completed action. We are to kill these things, and walk away from the corpses. But even when this is done, it does not mean that *all* our problems with lust will then vanish away. Paul also tells us in Romans that the duty of mortification of lust remains an ongoing one—

> For if ye live after the flesh, ye shall die: but if ye through the Spirit *do mortify* the deeds of the body, ye shall live. (Rom. 8:13)

This requirement is stated in the present tense; it remains a duty for any who have an unredeemed body. Christians are capable of giving way to sin and temporarily allowing that sin to do in them and with them what it ought not to do. If sin has *permanent* dominion in a man, then the man is unregenerate. As John teaches us, a man born of God does not sin habitually in such a way (1 Jn. 3:9).

Before regeneration, a man was dominated by the desires of the flesh. This dominion of the flesh we may call the "old man." When this old man is crucified with Christ, it is no longer a factor (Rom. 6:1–6). But while *reigning sin* is dead and gone, this does not mean that the corruptions of the flesh are gone. Christians sometimes find themselves doing corrupt things with their earthly bodies—so Paul says to knock it off and to mortify such practices. Put them to death, and walk away.

But he also teaches that we must defend our walk with God daily from this enemy within: "Let not sin therefore reign in your mortal body, that ye should obey it in the lusts thereof" (Rom. 6:12). Christians, whose old man has died with Christ, are told not to *let* sin reign. How would it be possible for a true Christian to let sin reign in his mortal body? When Paul says we should not obey it in *its* lusts, the Greek requires that the pronoun refer back to the phrase "mortal body." Sin reigns in a Christian when that Christian does what his mortal body tells him to. "Hey, would you take a look at *her!*" Resistance must continue as long as the body has desires which are contrary to the law of God, which is to say, until we die. We must set ourselves against these things *constantly.*

These lusts are not raging in someone else's members. As Christians, we must abstain from our *own* lusts. Before we were converted, we would conform to our former lusts in ignorance. Peter says, "Wherefore gird up the loins of your mind, be sober, and hope to the end for the grace that is to be brought unto you at the revelation of Jesus Christ; as obedient children, *not fashioning yourselves according to the former lusts* in your ignorance: but as he which hath called you is holy, so be ye holy in all manner of conversation" (1 Pet. 1:13–15). Peter is telling Christians to avoid conforming themselves to a pattern of lust. This is what they used to do, but they are to do so no longer. Now remember that his prohibition is delivered to *Christians.* Christians are told to refrain from doing something they are obviously capable of doing. The New Testament is filled with such warnings to *Christians.*

A few verses later, he tells Christians to abstain from their lusts: "Dearly beloved, I beseech you as strangers and pilgrims, *abstain from fleshly lusts*, which war against the soul" (1 Pet. 2:11). These lusts (*our* lusts) are at war with the soul (*our* souls). They are not a raging fire in somebody else's head. If that were the case, obedience to this command would be a piece of cake.

Scripture delivers these sorts of warnings to Christians again and again. When a believer finds himself allured by the world or the things in it, he is sinning. But he is not sinning in some bizarre, unheard of fashion. These lusts are a standard-issue problem. If someone gives way to these lusts, loving them, the love of the Father is not in him. But if someone claims that he does not have these lusts at all, then he is an unvarnished liar or a block of wood (1 Jn. 1:8–10)—

> Love not the world, neither the things that are in the world. If any man love the world, the love of the Father is not in him. For all that is in the world, the lust of the flesh, and

the lust of the eyes, and the pride of life, is not of the Father, but is of the world. And the world passeth away, and the lust thereof: but he that doeth the will of God abideth for ever. (1 Jn. 2:15–17)

One of the solutions presented to us in Scripture is the practice of thinking about our lusts in their proper context. In Colossians, Paul tells us to set our minds on things above—this would enable us to put to death our earthly members. We may put fornication to death because we have already died and our life is hidden with Christ in God. In this passage, John reminds us that the world is passing away, and all its lusts. We are to meditate on this. Lust is an evanescent, temporal thing. One hundred years ago, many thousands of men were just as lustful as they are today. At the time it was experienced, the lust seemed powerful and all-consuming. But where is that lust *now*? For that matter, where are *they* now? The peculiar clarity of mind, and resulting change of attitude, which comes after lust is satisfied provides no relief, only harshness. The reaction that follows the fulfillment of the lust is unlikely to be balanced—

> Howbeit he would not hearken unto her voice: but, being stronger than she, forced her, and lay with her. Then Amnon hated her exceedingly; so that the hatred wherewith he hated her was greater than the love wherewith he had loved her. And Amnon said unto her, Arise, be gone. (2 Sam. 13:14–15)

Christian men must seek another kind of clarity, and learn to see their lusts and desires in the light of eternal things. To meditate on our position in Christ is one preventative measure, and to consider the fleeting nature of sexual immorality is another. Yet another is remembering the fact that God *judges:*

> Marriage is honourable in all, and the bed undefiled: but whoremongers and adulterers God will judge. Let your conversation be without covetousness; and be content

with such things as ye have: for he hath said, I will never leave thee, nor forsake thee. (Heb. 13:4–5)

We see that the key to keeping the marriage bed undefiled is *contentment*. Because God will judge, a man is commanded to be content with what he *has*. His wife's breasts are not like those of Miss February. So? God will judge. She can't make his orgasms last forever like those hot little numbers in the videos do. So? God will judge—and He will not simply judge the sexual immorality. He will also judge men for believing lies about sexual impossibilities:

> Drink waters out of thine own cistern, and running waters out of thine own well. Let [not] thy fountains be dispersed abroad, and rivers of waters in the streets. Let them be only thine own, and not strangers' with thee. Let thy fountain be blessed: and rejoice with the wife of thy youth. Let her be as the loving hind and pleasant roe; let her breasts satisfy thee at all times; and be thou ravished always with her love. And why wilt thou, my son, be ravished with a strange woman, and embrace the bosom of a stranger? For the ways of man are before the eyes of the LORD, and he pondereth all his goings. (Prov. 5:15–21)

A man must be content with his wife's breasts—not some porn queen's breasts. Christian men are to be fully satisfied at home. Let *her* breasts satisfy you, Solomon says. To become aroused by viewing another woman and then satisfying that desire with his own wife is disobedience. He must be content because *God is watching* his eyes, his mind, his genitals, his heart. The Lord *ponders* all a man's paths—to the video store, the magazine rack, near a sexually provocative woman, etc. When he is home alone, God *watches* his thumb on the remote control. This is more than ample reason to be satisfied with the contents of his wife's blouse. And those men who are single, and who have no one at home, must learn, for the time being, to be content with *that*.

Speaking of believing lies, Peter tells us that one of the

weapons in the arsenal of false teachers is the spacious room their doctrine makes for lust—"For when they speak great swelling words of vanity, they allure through the lusts of the flesh, through much wantonness . . ." (2 Pet. 2:18). This allowance for lust is characteristic of doctrinal error— "But chiefly them that walk after the flesh in the lust of uncleanness, and despise government" (2 Pet. 2:10). Many Christians know what it is like to live in this fashion. They used to be that way prior to conversion. Paul reminds the Ephesians of this—"among whom also we all had our conversation in times past in the lusts of our flesh, fulfilling the desires of the flesh and of the mind" (Eph. 2:3). He sternly reminds them that their former habits must be put away: ". . . that ye put off concerning the former conversation the old man, which is corrupt according to the deceitful lusts" (Eph. 4:22). Notice here that lusts are not just wrong, they are deceitful *liars*. The endless pleasure promised is not delivered, and the pain and heartache that follows was never mentioned.

Many believers have been brought out of a world which runs on the gasoline of lust: "For we ourselves also were sometimes foolish, disobedient, deceived, serving divers lusts and pleasures, living in malice and envy, hateful, and hating one another" (Tit. 3:3). Why on earth would we want to climb back into that snake pit? Nothing can come of it but the kind of suffering especially adapted to the sexual meathead—"The righteousness of the upright will deliver them, but the unfaithful will be caught by their lust" (Prov. 11:6 NKJV).

Here is the problem: Lust demands from a finite thing (sexual pleasure) what only the Infinite can provide—"Hell and destruction are never full; so the *eyes of man* are *never satisfied*" (Prov. 27:20). When men are in the grip of prolonged lust they are soon dissatisfied with normal sexual pleasure and begin looking around for other things which will expand their sexual horizons. This is the source of all perversions and fetishes. The whole world becomes a sexual partner, and like a mongrel dog on some hapless postman's leg, they begin humping everything in sight—

> Wherefore God also gave them up to uncleanness through the lusts of their own hearts, to dishonour their own bodies between themselves. . . . For this cause God gave them up unto vile affections: for even their women did change the natural use into that which is against nature: and likewise also the men, leaving the natural use of the woman, burned in their lust one toward another; men with men working that which is unseemly, and receiving in themselves that recompence of their error which was meet. (Rom. 1:24, 26–27)

When God determines to judge a people, He gives them up in this way. Burning lust that overflows is not an example of men getting away from God (as they like to tell themselves); it is an example of the wrath of God catching up with men. The natural use of the woman is abandoned, and the pursuit of the unnatural begins. But those Christians who react with dismay to the horrors of fruitless sodomy must realize that this awful disobedience has come from *our* toleration of *our* sexual disobedience. We must realize that the defiant subculture of sodomy was not caused by the position of the moon; it was caused by widespread heterosexual disobedience, which at some point naturally and inexorably overflows its banks. So—"Let us walk honestly, as in the day; not in rioting and drunkenness, not in chambering and wantonness, not in strife and envying. But put ye on the Lord Jesus Christ, and make not provision for the flesh, to fulfil the lusts thereof" (Rom. 13:13–14).

When we walk away from sexual sin, we are also walking away from a host of other entanglements—"From whence come wars and fightings among you? Come they not hence, even of your lusts that war in your members? Ye lust, and have not: ye kill, *and desire to have*, and cannot obtain: ye fight and war, yet ye have not, because ye ask not" (Jas. 4:1–2). This kind of desire for pleasure, that is, lust, is suicidal. Those who worship sexual pleasure receive, in the long run, the destruction of the thing they worship. Wisdom tells us in Proverbs that all who hate her love death (Prov. 8:36). Those who hate sexual wisdom love sexual death.

Peter teaches us that Christ offers a way of escape from these corruptions of our lusts, and our indulgence of them. But until the resurrection, there is no relief from the *presence* of them:

> Grace and peace be multiplied unto you through the knowledge of God, and of Jesus our Lord, according as his divine power hath given unto us *all things that pertain unto life and godliness*, through the knowledge of him that hath called us to glory and virtue: whereby are given unto us exceeding great and precious promises: that by these ye might be partakers of the divine nature, *having escaped the corruption that is in the world through lust.* And beside this, giving all diligence, add to your faith virtue; and to virtue knowledge; and to knowledge *temperance*; and to temperance patience; and to patience godliness; and to godliness brotherly kindness; and to brotherly kindness charity. For if these things be in you, and abound, they make you that ye shall neither be barren nor unfruitful in the knowledge of our Lord Jesus Christ. (2 Pet. 1:2–8)

This escape from corruption is genuine, but it is not yet completed. When we receive our resurrection bodies, we will no longer be troubled by our lusts. But until then, we must expect their presence with us daily, and we must expect, through the grace of Christ, genuine victory in subduing them. Because there will be no temptation in heaven, this world is an opportunity for us to grow, fight, and struggle against sin in such a way as to show our devotion to Christ. Learning to war against our lusts provides a wonderful opportunity to show such devotion. So the Bible teaches both—an ongoing struggle with our lusts, and the genuine possibility of subduing those lusts.

In addition to what has already been mentioned, I want

to outline a biblical response to the problem of lust which will apply equally to men who are single and men who have a wife. After that, I will include a discussion pertinent to the peculiar situation of each.

Our first duty is to learn the gospel. The grace of God is manifested in the world through the gospel: "For the grace of God that bringeth salvation hath appeared to all men, *teaching* us that, *denying ungodliness and worldly lusts*, we should live soberly, righteously, and godly, in this present world" (Tit. 2:11–12). The NIV renders this as the grace of God teaching us to say *no* to ungodliness. As we learn the gospel, it teaches us how to deny ungodliness and worldly lusts. This means that we must give ourselves to learn what the Bible teaches about the grace of God in Christ. Learning the gospel and growing in the grace of the gospel mean much more than nodding at the appropriate places in some modern, truncated presentation of what is thought to be the gospel. The gospel is much more than "receive Jesus into your heart." Given the version of the gospel peddled in much of modern evangelicalism, it is not surprising that we have not learned to deny much of anything.

Related to this, as sunlight is related to sunrise, we must learn what the Bible teaches about sanctification, particularly the relationship between the Spirit of God within us and the remaining lusts within us. That relationship is one of *war*: "This I say then, walk in the Spirit, and ye shall not fulfil the lust of the flesh. For the flesh lusteth against the Spirit, and the Spirit against the flesh: and these are contrary the one to the other: so that ye cannot do the things that ye would" (Gal. 5:16–17). Why are we sometimes frustrated in our desire for personal holiness? The answer is this war between the flesh and the Spirit.

In learning this, we come to understand that Christ has redeemed our bodies and that He therefore owns them. He has united Himself to us covenantally, and because a sexual union with a prostitute involves another kind of union, someone who sins sexually is sinning against the temple of the Holy Spirit. This principle is not limited to consorting with prostitutes. All sexual sin is involved. But contrary to popular opinion, the verse about sinning against this temple applies *only* to sexual sin. All other sins a man commits are outside his body, but this one is against his own body. Further, when a man sins sexually, he is vandalizing the property of another. Our bodies are not our own; we were bought with a price—

> All things are lawful unto me, but all things are not expedient: all things are lawful for me, but I will not be brought under the power of any. Meats for the belly, and the belly for meats: but God shall destroy both it and them. *Now the body is not for fornication, but for the Lord*; and the Lord for the body. And God hath both raised up the Lord, and will also raise up us by his own power. Know ye not that your bodies are the members of Christ? shall I then take the members of Christ, and make them the members of an harlot? God forbid. What? know ye not that he which is joined to an harlot is one body? for two, saith he, shall be one flesh. But he that is joined unto the Lord is one spirit. *Flee fornication*. Every sin that a man doeth is without the body; but *he that committeth fornication sinneth against his own body*. What? know ye not that your body is the temple of the Holy Ghost which is in you, which ye have of God, and ye are not your own? For *ye are bought with a price*: therefore glorify God in your body, and in your spirit, which are God's. (1 Cor. 6:12–20)

Third, we must learn the value of discipline and suffering. Someone who is lazy and self-indulgent in other areas will find it much easier to be lazy and self-indulgent in the sexual area—

> Forasmuch then as Christ hath suffered for us in the flesh, arm yourselves likewise with the same mind: *for he that hath suffered in the flesh hath ceased from sin*; that he no longer should live the rest of his time *in the flesh to the lusts of men*, but to the will of God. For the time past of our life

may suffice us to have wrought the will of the Gentiles, *when we walked in lasciviousness, lusts*, excess of wine, revellings, banquetings, and abominable idolatries. (1 Pet. 4:1–3)

Peter says plainly here that suffering in the body is an effective weapon against lust. By this he does not mean asceticism—Paul tells us *that* has no value in checking sensual indulgence (Col. 2:23). Rather, Peter is referring to suffering for the sake of Christ, and I think we also may include the practice of bodily discipline for the sake of Christ (1 Cor. 9:27; 1 Tim. 4:8). Self-control learned in one area transfers to another. A man who has self-control in one area will have greater success applying it in another than a man who has self-control in no areas. Self-indulgence in one area is difficult to limit to that area.

The fourth duty is to learn from the bad examples set before us in Scripture:

> Now these things were *our examples*, to the intent we should not *lust* after evil things, as they also *lusted*. Neither be ye idolaters, as were some of them; as it is written, The people sat down to eat and drink, and rose up to play. Neither let us commit fornication, as some of them committed, and fell in one day three and twenty thousand. (1 Cor. 10:6–8)

More than one Israelite man went to worship the golden calf because there was a good prospect there for getting laid. It sort of gave the "golden calf theology" that little extra appeal. God struck twenty-three thousand of them down because of it. We should be well acquainted with God's treatment of them, along with His destruction of Sodom and Gomorrah, His judgment in the Flood, and so forth. These things were written for us as examples, and apparently God thinks them to be *effective* examples. We must know them and meditate on them.

The fifth thing men must do is run away—flee the occasions of sin. When the wife of Potiphar grabbed Joseph so that he would have sex with her, he fled. She said, "Lie with me" (Gen. 39:7). He said, "Seeya" (Gen. 39:12). Paul also tells Timothy to *run away*: "*Flee* also youthful lusts: but follow righteousness, faith, charity, peace with them that call on the Lord out of a pure heart" (2 Tim. 2:22). In the passage noted earlier he tells the Corinthians to flee sexual immorality (1 Cor. 6:18). Connected with this is the practice of running *toward* righteousness, faith, love, and peace. You cannot fight something with nothing. Those who want to fight the temptation to watch some topless women on HBO by sitting on the couch with the remote in hand are likely to be disappointed. *Flee*.

The specific help offered to married men in Scripture, that of a satisfying sexual relationship, is not available to single men. Consequently, the advice offered here may seem simplistic, but I believe it to be the biblical approach. If a single man is gifted with celibacy (1 Cor. 7:7), then the whole point is moot, and he is probably not reading this book. If he does not have that gift, but is maintaining his sexual purity with success, then he is probably doing what has been outlined above, and he should continue to do it. At the same time, he knows that in the long run he needs a woman, and he should seek the Lord's gift of marriage for him. The best thing he can do is to prepare for marriage by learning to be a godly Christian in his current condition and working hard to provide in advance for his future wife.

A man who does not have the gift of celibacy, and who is struggling to maintain his purity should get married at the first opportunity. Paul comes right to the point. His teaching had application to a peculiar situation in the first century, but the principle remains constant. Marriage is better than burning—"But if they cannot contain, let them marry: for it is better to marry than to burn" (1 Cor. 7:9).

Those things which a young man must do to prepare for marriage, this young man must do with all diligence. He must work hard so that he will be able to provide financially for a wife and children, and he should marry at the first opportunity. But if for some reason marriage is not practical, and immorality *is* available, then he should seek out some biblical accountability—either his father or the elders of his church. In the last resort, he should seek the accountability of peers.

But what about his sexual behavior in the meantime, before marriage? Probably the most practical question facing young single men is the question of masturbation, which will be addressed in greater detail in a later chapter. Suffice it to say for the present that masturbation should not be considered as a "cure" for lust in the same way that a good marriage is.

But getting married is no *automatic* solution to the problem of lust. In a fallen world, God does intend for a healthy sexual relationship within marriage to provide protection against temptation. But the process of learning how this is done takes thought and study. There is a right way and wrong way to take a wife sexually. The wrong way provides no relief whatever from the assaults of lust:

> For this is the will of God, even your sanctification, that ye should abstain from fornication: *that every one of you should know how to possess his vessel in sanctification and honour; not in the lust of concupiscence, even as the Gentiles which know not God*: that no man go beyond and defraud his brother in any matter: because that the Lord is the avenger of all such, as we also have forewarned you and testified. For God hath not called us unto uncleanness, but unto holiness. He therefore that despiseth, despiseth not man, but God, who hath also given unto us his holy Spirit. (1 Thes. 4:3–8)

A man who thinks that marriage simply means free sex, and that he now "gets it" whenever he "wants it" has not learned what God wants him to learn. In every way a Christian man is to treat his wife like a lady. But the thoughtless man is not making love to a wife; he is masturbating in someone else's presence. One writer spoke memorably of the fact that some men make love to a woman the way an orangutuan might play the violin. This kind of sexual bonehead is quickly frustrated with his "frigid" wife and is off looking for females more to his liking. He soon finds them in pornography: women who are willing, for a fee, to pretend that they are not women. These women give him what he wants, when he wants it, how he wants it, and he never has to deal with the troublesome problems caused by *somebody else*. When a man approaches his wife in the "passionate lust" of the Gentiles, he soon discovers that the marriage bed is not enough for him. He must go somewhere else, or supplement what he has with pornography, or try to import some other kind of serious weirdness into his lovemaking.

CHAPTER THREE

Fornication

In this chapter, I am using the word *fornication* in its English sense and not as a strict rendering of the Greek *porneias*, which means sexual uncleanness. In our language, fornication is sexual activity in the absence of a marriage covenant, while adultery is sexual activity contrary to an established marriage covenant. It is my purpose here simply to address the sexual behavior of a man with a woman when there is no covenant relationship. The biblical use of fornication is broader than the use I am employing here, but at the same time this English use of the word is certainly included in the biblical prohibitions. Some of the other things included in the biblical prohibition of *porneias* are addressed in other chapters.

When a man drifts into sexual sin, he usually drifts farther and farther, and when he does so, rationalizations for his behavior are not long in coming. When it is a Christian man involved, the rationalizations are used by him prior to the sexual encounter, everything becomes clear to him as soon as he climaxes, and then it takes a few days for the sexual fog to start to build up again. When it does, the rationalizations start in again. The best way to prevent such self-justifying rationalization is to know the teaching of the Word of God on the subject, in pointed detail.

Generally, under the heading of fornication, I am addressing any behavior involving two people—a man and a woman not married to one another—and behavior which would usually result in an orgasm for the man. In any such situation, the man is fornicating whether or not he has intercourse with the woman (although, of course, such intercourse is also fornication). Specifically, I am addressing heavy petting with a girlfriend or fiancee (or anybody else) to the point of climax, frequenting massage parlors in order to get a hand job, getting a lap dance and masturbating later, fellatio or oral sex, *coitus interruptus*, and complete sexual intercourse. I am sure I did not include every possible thing, so the reader should consider those included now. When confronted with our sin, we all tend to become technicians of the language, saying that whether there was sin or not all depends upon what *is* is. We invent arbitrary rules for ourselves to allow for some activities and exclude others. But for our purposes here, fornication is any kind of unmarried fooling around, and every reasonable person knows what fooling around is, with no room for justifications.

To all such, the apostle Paul says:

> Know ye not that the unrighteous shall not inherit the kingdom of God? Be not deceived: neither *fornicators*, nor idolaters, nor adulterers, nor effeminate, nor abusers of themselves with mankind, nor thieves, nor covetous, nor drunkards, nor revilers, nor extortioners, shall inherit the kingdom of God. (1 Cor. 6:9–10)

Fornicators do not go to heaven. They do not inherit the kingdom of God. They would be well advised to quit it. The Bible sets before us the clear possibility of deliverance from sexual temptation, including the temptation to fornicate. Paul goes on to say that such deliverance had come to the Corinthians: "And such were some of you: but ye are washed, but ye are sanctified, but ye are justified in the name of the Lord Jesus, and by the Spirit of our God" (v. 11). This passage is usually applied to homosexuals, seeking to show them that there really is a way out of

their perversion—does not the apostle say that some of
the Corinthians had been homosexual, and that now they
were not?

This is quite right, and it is a good application, but we
sometimes miss another obvious point of encouragement.
Whether or not homosexual temptation is genetic, heterosexual tempation most certainly is genetic. A man who is
not gifted with celibacy, but who is morally required to be
celibate for the time being, is in a difficult place. When
women are available and willing, this is a hard sin to avoid,
especially if the man in question has been accustomed to
fornication and is trying to break an established habit. Paul
says here that, among the Corinthians, a number of them
had been delivered from fornication. By the grace of God,
the thing is possible.

And the Corinthians knew something about how to
overcome sin in this area. We sometimes assume that the
decadence of our times somehow makes avoidance of fornication extraordinarily difficult. But our problems are
nothing compared to the problems which faced a young
Corinthian Christian man. The city of Corinth was re-
nowned for its immorality, and throughout the Roman
Empire the verb "to corinthianize" meant "to corrupt."
The Temple of Aphrodite was there, dedicated to Venus or
Aphrodite, the goddess of sexual love. Her temple was
staffed with a thousand priestesses, that is to say, sacred
whores. (Incidentally, these women were shorn, which
sheds some light on Paul's teaching later in Corinthians on
head coverings for women.)

Fornication was not only easy to get into in Corinth, it
was a city in which fornication was considered a sacred
duty. Copulating with a designated whore was considered
an act of worship. Imagine the pressure and temptation on
a young man coming out of this kind of life. And Paul says,
"And such were some of you."

The demands of the body are not the source of our
ethical knowledge. Paul says that everything is lawful for

him, but this does not mean that everything is helpful. When he says "everything" he of course does not mean those things expressly prohibited by God—he means those things allowed by the law of God, but which are not for that reason encouraged. Everything is lawful, but he does not want to be subordinated to anything, not even to something which is lawful in itself (v. 12). For example, he says that the stomach and food were made for each other, but this was not intended as a permanent state of affairs. A day is coming when both stomach and food will be destroyed (v. 13).

Food was made for the body, but will one day be destroyed. By way of contrast, fornication was *not* made for the body. The body was not made for fornication. Contrary to one of the most common lies in this regard, sexual activity with a woman outside a covenant is *not* "natural"— "Now the body is not for fornication, but for the Lord; and the Lord for the body" (v. 13).The fact that it seems natural to us simply shows how fallen our race is. A good lunch serves the body, which Paul agrees with in a qualified way, and so it seems to us that a good lay would do the same thing. Many unbelievers think that sexual intercourse is just another physical action—like scratching an itch, or drinking water when you are thirsty. God, the Creator, the one who should know, says that fornication is *unnatural*. It does not compare to the act of eating at all. Food and stomach are lawful companions, albeit temporary ones. In the resurrection, we will not be tied to food in the way we are now. God will raise us up to a new state of affairs (v. 14). In the meantime, we should have a disciplined and careful approach to food. But fornication is in another category altogether—it is not even a temporary blessing to the body.

God designed the human body for Himself. In His grace, He has brought us into a covenantal union with Christ. We are one with Christ through faith, which provides the basis of Paul's following argument against fornication. Some in the church at Corinth were still frequenting brothels and did not see the incongruity. Although some in the church had been delivered, we must note that some had *not* been. Sexual sin with prostitutes was common enough in that church to warrant teaching on the subject by the apostle. Because the body was designed to be united to Christ, and because through the gospel, it had been united with Christ, this meant that what that body did with harlots would result in a very real desecration:

> Know ye not that your bodies are the members of Christ? Shall I then take the members of Christ, and make them the members of an harlot? God forbid. What? know ye not that he which is joined to an harlot is one body? for two, saith he, shall be one flesh. But he that is joined unto the Lord is one spirit. (vv. 15–17)

In other words, because the believing man is united with Christ, is one with Him, if he then engages in behavior which also makes him one with a whore, He has involved Christ in his sin. Sexual activity always results in a one flesh union. The passage quoted by Paul is from Genesis and was originally speaking of marriage, and it is quoted elsewhere by him and is applied to marriage (Eph. 5:31). But a one flesh union occurs whether or not a marriage has been contracted. There is no incongruity between the holy covenantal union with Christ on the one hand and holy sex within the bounds of holy matrimony on the other. There *is* a fundamental incongruity between this holiness in Christ and cavorting with a hooker.

But Paul continues with his argument. Sexual sin is not the worst of sins, but in some respects we may consider it the most complicated of sins. All dirt should be washed off our hands, but pine sap is harder to get off. Sexual sin *entangles* in a way that other sins do not—

> Flee fornication. Every sin that a man doeth is without the body; but he that committeth fornication sinneth against his own body. (v. 18)

In the verses that follow, Paul mentions that we are the

Temple of the Holy Spirit. That phrase, lifted out of context, has been used to urge Christians to refrain from refined sugar, sedentary lifestyles, and, of course, big stinky cigars. But Paul says specifically that he is only talking about sexual sin here. Other sins are outside the body, but fornication is not. This would include chopping a finger off with an axe. Poor stewardship, bad idea, and all that, but it is not a defilement of the Temple. *That* is accomplished through fornication.

This is why Paul says that we are to flee fornication. This is not a mindless reaction; rather, we are to understand the nature of the temptation, the nature of the danger, and consequently run like mad from it. Notice again that fornication is not "natural" or "healthy." A man who sleeps with a woman who is not his wife is not just sinning against God, but is also sinning against his own body. Immorality is an insult to the body. Those who live in this way will continue to haul down upon their own heads all the natural consequences of unnatural behavior. How is it that a man can make love to his wife thousands of times over the course of forty years and not be at risk for any sexually transmitted diseases, while another man can have three one-night stands and find himself crawling with sexually transmitted pests? And tell us again which behavior is more *natural?*—

> What? know ye not that your body is the temple of the Holy Ghost which is in you, which ye have of God, and ye are not your own? For ye are bought with a price: therefore glorify God in your body, and in your spirit, which are God's. (vv. 19–20)

Peter tells us that we are living stones, being built up into the Temple of God. Since we are a kingdom of priests, since we have been gathered togethered into a holy assembly, it is an act of desecration even to bring a prostitute into *indirect* union with such holy things. She does not belong there.

But the argument does not rest upon appeals to incongruity alone. Paul says that the way the Corinthian Christians got into this union with Christ was through His purchase of them. They were bought with a price; they are not their own. The contrast, remember, is between a holy union with Christ and an unholy union with a whore. The whore is purchased, which is why a man feels he has a right to have intercourse with her. But Paul says here that there has been a prior purchase. A man cannot buy a whore for himself because he has no ownership claim on anything. If he purchases a woman, he can only do it as a delegate, with someone else's money. And whose money might it be? Of course the answer is that it is Christ's money. And if he goes in to her, to use the Old Testament euphemism, then whose body is performing the act of copulation? Of course the answer is that Christ purchased his body with His own blood, and so properly it belongs to Him. Consequently, an immoral Christian is fornicating with misappropriated or stolen property.

A man must recognize that he belongs to Christ, both body and spirit. The duty which follows from this is the need to glorify God in both. Marital lovemaking glorifies God (Heb. 13:4). In fact, just a few verses down, Paul shows that one important way to flee fornication is to run into the arms of a woman (1 Cor. 7:2). But all acts of fornication and uncleanness do not glorify God—and cannot.

To fear the Lord is to hate evil—and to do so in the way the Lord does. We sometimes rank sins, stacking them up in our own private hierarchies, thinking that because *we* tolerate and understand some sin or other, then God must think of it in the same indulgent way. But this is not the case and is certainly not the case with fornication. God places the sin in some pretty bad company:

> And even as they did not like to retain God in their knowledge, God gave them over to a reprobate mind, to do those things which are not convenient; being filled with all

unrighteousness, *fornication*, wickedness, covetousness, maliciousness; full of envy, murder. . . ." (Rom. 1:28–29)

Fornication is a companion to many other sins. As much as a young man might want his fornication to be contained and isolated, with complete respectability being possible in other areas, it appears that he cannot have his desire. It is not possible; sins are like grapes, and come in bunches—

> But if ye be led of the Spirit, ye are not under the law. Now the works of the flesh are manifest, which are these; adultery, *fornication*, uncleanness, lasciviousness, idolatry, witchcraft, hatred, variance, emulations, wrath, strife, seditions, heresies, envyings, murders, drunkenness, revellings, and such like: of the which I tell you before, as I have also told you in time past, that they which do such things shall not inherit the kingdom of God. (Gal. 5:18–21)

One way of life includes fornication—and all the rest of its companions. Another way of life, the way of the Spirit, goes down another road entirely. One path leads to the kingdom of God, and the other one does not.

The writers of the New Testament place sins together in so many "lists," not because they had a strange passion for categorization, but because the sins go together. Whenever any frame of mind which resists God is tolerated, the logic of that position will work out into resistance across the board—

> For I fear, lest, when I come, I shall not find you such as I would, and that I shall be found unto you such as ye would not: lest there be debates, envyings, wraths, strifes, backbitings, whisperings, swellings, tumults: and lest, when I come again, my God will humble me among you, and that I shall bewail many which have sinned already, and have not repented of the uncleanness and *fornication* and lasciviousness which they have committed. (2 Cor. 12:20–21)

When a man wanders into certain beds, he does not find peace there. In the sixties, that time of sexual infantilism, we were frequently urged to make love, not war. The assumption was that lovemaking was a *peaceful* activity, regardless of who you were in the hay with. But James tells us where war comes from—warring desires:

> From whence come wars and fightings among you? come they not hence, *even of your lusts that war in your members?* Ye lust, and have not: ye kill, and desire to have, and cannot obtain: ye fight and war, yet ye have not, because ye ask not. Ye ask, and receive not, because ye ask amiss, that ye may consume it upon your lusts. Ye adulterers and adulteresses, know ye not that the friendship of the world is enmity with God? whosoever therefore will be a friend of the world is the enemy of God. Do ye think that the scripture saith in vain, The spirit that dwelleth in us lusteth to envy? But he giveth more grace. Wherefore he saith, God resisteth the proud, but giveth grace unto the humble. Submit yourselves therefore to God. Resist the devil, and he will flee from you. (Jas. 4:1–7)

Sexual revolutions must necessarily end in blood. And to consider the truth of this we do not need to look off in the distance at all the trouble caused by Helen of Troy. James tells us that men war and fight because of lust. On whom they make war may vary, but the result is the same. The sexual laxity of our nation, to take an example close to home, has resulted to date in 38 million abortions. Considered from another angle, that means 38 million orgasms, 38 million temporarily satisfied men, 38 million good times in the sack that ended badly for the inconvenient byproduct. In short, millions of men thought that someone else's life was a reasonable price to pay for the pleasure of getting off. When lust is inflamed and encouraged, as it is in our nation, it cannot be detached from conflict that comes to blood. And fighting in our midst comes directly from losing the fight within our members.

James tells us that our spirit tends toward this lust, but

God gives more grace to those who are submitted to Him. Our spirit tends toward friendship with the world, which amounts to enmity with God. A flirtacious woman, a low-cut blouse, tight jeans, and a come-on look are all invitations to show contempt for God.

And when we show contempt for God, we soon discover that He is not the frail deity many have assumed Him to be. It is not as though He does not know how to respond when we show contempt for Him. The God of the Bible, as one writer put it aptly, is no buttercup. When we set ourselves against Him in enmity, He responds in judgment:

> Now these things were our examples, to the intent we should not lust after evil things, as they also lusted. Neither be ye idolaters, as were some of them; as it is written, The people sat down to eat and drink, and rose up to play. *Neither let us commit fornication, as some of them committed, and fell in one day three and twenty thousand.* (1 Cor. 10:6–8)

The stories of the Bible are given to us so that we might take warning. The God of the Bible judges the sin of fornication both within history and at the end of history. Within history, He visits a man with sexual diseases, conflict, guilt, turmoil, lack of peace and satisfaction, a miserable family, and death. At the culmination of history, He closes the gates of everlasting life in the face of those who did not repent of their fornications.

In short, we have to say that God does not take a "boys will be boys" approach.

CHAPTER FOUR

Adultery

As Jesus applies the law of God, He continues the same pattern that we see throughout all Scripture. Obedience to the law is never a matter of external conformity; it is a question of heart loyalty. Put another way, the well-respected and externally pious tend to think about *sins*. The godly are constrained by the teaching of Christ to think about *sin*—the condition of sinfulness, the fountainhead of all sins.

Before considering adultery as a sin commited in real time, we must consider adultery as an incipient inclination of the heart. Jesus teaches us that all adultery *begins* in the heart:

> Ye have heard that it was said by them of old time, Thou shalt not commit adultery: but I say unto you, that whosoever looketh on a woman to lust after her hath committed adultery with her already in his heart. And if thy right eye offend thee, pluck it out, and cast it from thee: for it is profitable for thee that one of thy members should perish, and not that thy whole body should be cast into hell. And if thy right hand offend thee, cut it off, and cast it from thee: for it is profitable for thee that one of thy members should perish, and not that thy whole body should be cast into hell. (Mt. 5:27–30)

The problem is one of heart rebellion. Jesus applies the law of God in a way which "decent" people do not

like. His application of the law makes *all* men adulterers,
and His teaching on the subject is plain. We see this principle when Christ teaches about money. He said that men
love to justify themselves before other men, but *God knows
the heart* (Lk. 16:15). What a fearful thought! God knows
the heart. And what does He see there? Among other
things, He sees a good deal of adultery (Mt. 15:19; cf. Mk.
7:21). The source of sins is *sin*. The source of sin is the
human heart.

This should be a thing of horror to us. Christ does not
just say in this passage that real adultery is a matter of the
heart. He says that such inner adultery is of immense im-
portance to the sinner. How important is it?

Rather than fall under the judgment of God for sin, the
sinner should prefer self-mutilation. If removing eyes and
hands would remove sin, then sin is serious enough to do
exactly that. Because the context of this passage is the teaching about adultery on one side and then divorce on the
other, Christ is clearly alluding to the preferability of self-
castration to that of facing the wrath of God because of the
demands of lust. But of course the problem is that self-
mutilation will not work to restrain sin. Neither will asceticism (Col. 2:23).

What is the offending member? What brings us to sin?
What produces sin in us? What must therefore be cut off?
The answer is that the offending member is *the human heart*.
The doctrine is that a man must have a new heart *or he will
die*.

The solution is regeneration. We must get the doctrine
of regeneration straight in our minds. A tremendous
amount of mischief has resulted from confusion at this
point. We are not born again because we have repented and
believed. Rather, we have repented and believed because
God has given us the new birth. If the old heart is capable
of repentance and belief, *then a man does not need a new
heart*. He simply needs to continue to improve the old one.

What does God promise through the prophet?

A new heart also will I give you, and a new spirit will I put within you: and I will take away the stony heart out of your flesh, and I will give you an heart of flesh. And I will put my spirit within you, and cause you to walk in my statutes, and ye shall keep my judgments, and do them. (Ezek. 36:26–27)

Who will do this? God is the only one who can, and that is something He promises to do for His people.

Jesus calls His followers to a genuine submission to the law of God. If we cannot, then we must cry out for a new heart. If we are believers who have drifted into compromise, then we must confess our sin to Him. He is faithful and just to forgive. Our new hearts enable us to look *to Him* for all our righteousness. True purity is found only there.

We must remember that sin muddles. It follows from this that sexual sin muddles sexually. So even though we live in a sex-crazed society, this does not mean we understand sex or sexual morality. The "openness" advocated by so many actually blurs the understanding. In such a situation, God's law illumines; disobedience results not only in sexual *immorality*, but also in sexual immaturity, ignorance, and imbecility.

The biblical requirement with regard to marriage is very plain: "Thou shalt not commit adultery" (Exod. 20:14). A husband who wants his home to be built on a biblical foundation must be very clear about the nature and requirements of this commandment. But a man who is only aware of the content of the command and is unfamiliar with the rest of the Bible's teaching on the subject is condemning himself to a hopeless existence—trapped between two worlds. He knows (he thinks) what he is supposed to avoid doing. But he does not know the range of passages which give him the necessary grace with regard to his motives. This means that he has an understanding of the rigor of God's standard without a grasp of the strength of God's kindness and grace, which is not a good place to be.

Obedience to God's sexual law is very important, and so we need to understand the motives to purity which God sets down in His Word. Job describes adultery as "wickedness" and "iniquity deserving of judgment" (Job 31:11). As we accept this judgment, we may be grateful that Scripture sets many godly incentives before us to keep us sexually pure. The Bible does not command us to stay away from sexually desirable women and then leave us to figure out on our own how such an impossible mission might be accomplished.

The first biblical motive is the fear of God—"The mouth of a strange woman is a deep pit: he that is *abhorred by the Lord* shall fall therein" (Prov. 22:14). We tend to think of adultery as getting away from God, when it is actually being captured by Him so that He might display His abhorrence of the sin by judging the one who fell into it. Joseph appeals to this principle as he resists seduction by the wife of Potiphar—"How then can I do this great wickedness, and sin against *God?*" (Gen. 39:9). God *witnesses* every sexual disobedience: "And I will come near to you for judgment; and I will be a swift witness against . . . adulterers" (Mal. 3:5; cf. Jer. 29:23). God judges sexual sin, and those who fear Him know this. A man thinks he is safe when he has gotten the woman safely past the desk clerk. But the holy God is present in the room where he is committing his adultery; He sees and knows all things.

A second godly motivation is the simple desire for salvation—"Know ye not that the unrighteous *shall not inherit* the kingdom of God? Be not deceived: neither *fornicators*, nor idolaters, nor *adulterers*, nor effeminate, nor abusers of themselves with mankind . . ." (1 Cor. 6:9). In Hebrews 13:4, we are bluntly told that fornicators and adulterers *God will judge.*

The Bible is very plain about this: "Her guests are in the depths of hell" (Prov. 9:18) A man cannot simultaneously want the salvation of God, and desire to remain in the sin from which God saves. Men who believe in God should know how much God hates this sin. Under the economy of the Old Testament, the offense was a captial offense—and not a mere sexual pecadillo: "And the man that committeth adultery with another man's wife, even he that committeth adultery with his neighbour's wife, the adulterer and the adulteress shall surely be put to death" (Lev. 20:10). Certainly an adulterer is worthy of death; a man who will betray his wife will betray anyone and anything. Adultery is treason against the family, and God hates it. Further, the capital punishment levied against this sin was only the beginning of the judgment—"Her house is the way to hell, going down to the chambers of death" (Prov. 7:27).

A third motivation is the love of a good wife. The godly husband is commanded to *rejoice* in his wife sexually (Prov. 5:18). The marriage bed is *honorable* (Heb. 13:4); the power of a biblical (i.e., good) sexual relationship is tremendous. But the marriage bed cannot be considered honorable unless we *honor* it. And if we honor it, we cannot drift to those competitive things which would dishonor it—"Many waters cannot quench love, neither can the flood drown it. If a man would give all the substance of his house for love, it would be utterly contemned" (Song 8:7). We should have contempt for those things which offer themselves to us instead of the love waiting at home. One of the great provisions that God has made to keep a man home is the goodness of the bed in that home. A wise man who loves the peaches at home does not want to shake any other trees.

We should also be motivated by fear of slavery and moral stupidity—

> For they shall eat, but not have enough: they shall commit whoredom, and shall not increase: because they have left off to take heed to the Lord. Whoredom and wine and new wine *take away the heart.* (Hos. 4:10–11)

When a man falls into adultery, he is falling into a prison. If he sees and recognizes this, he should fear it. If he does not, then his absence of fear is nothing but the mark of a fool.

By avoiding adultery, the godly man is also concerned to preserve his human dignity. Scripture repeatedly compares men in the grip of this sin to brute beasts (Jer. 5:8). Man is not like a beast because he shares with them a sexual nature; he is like them when he is driven by it. Sex is not bestial, but unthinking sex is always bestial—

> But these, as *natural brute beasts*, made to be taken and destroyed, speak evil of the things that they understand not; and shall utterly perish in their own corruption; and shall receive the reward of unrighteousness, as they that count it pleasure to riot in the day time. (2 Pet. 2:12–13)

Jude says something very similar: "But these speak evil of those things which they know not: but what they know naturally, *as brute beasts*, in those things they corrupt themselves" (Jude 10). An unreasoning dog does not suffer from having had multiple sexual partners. But a man who degrades himself to this level does. It is no contempt to say that a beast is a beast, but a man who bears the image of God and yet treats sex as a mere biological phenomenon is degraded and blind.

Here is yet another biblical motivation to purity: reputation. The Bible does not disparage a concern for reputation—

> But whoso committeth adultery with a woman lacketh understanding: he that doeth it destroyeth his own soul. A wound and *dishonour shall he get*; and *his reproach shall not be wiped away*. (Prov. 6:32–33)

"What will people say?" is a perfectly good question, and a question which more men ought to ask. As Moses reminded the people of Israel in another context, be sure your sin will find you out (Num. 32:23). Of course, this motivation considered alone is inadequate and by itself can be entirely consistent with unvarnished hypocrisy. But at the same time, the Bible teaches this as a true and effective motivation when placed among others. Shame is not honorable in itself, but it at least reflects a memory of honor.

As we considered earlier, a man should also be concerned about possible financial consequences—

> For by means of a whorish woman a man is brought *to a piece of bread*: and the adulteress will hunt for the precious life. (Prov. 6:26; cf. 5:10)

And we should remember the younger brother in Christ's parable reduced himself to pig food by squandering his heritage on whores (Lk. 15:30). Immorality is expensive. This is the result of a combination of factors, but one obvious consideration is that a man in the grip of lust has very low sales resistence. Once the desire has him by the throat, he is in no position to calculate rationally.

The motivations to avoid adultery are manifold. In the grip of carnal reasoning, many men want to tolerate the age-old double standard. Men are expected to sow a few wild oats, and women are expected to be sexually virtuous. Of course, the double-standard is not taught in the Bible— God has always required the same sexual obedience from men and women both. When adultery was committed, the law of God required that both man and woman be executed.

Nevertheless, the double-standard has been around for a long time. In Genesis 38, an awful sexual tangle is related. Judah arranged a marriage between his son Er and a woman named Tamar. Er was wicked so God killed him. Judah's other son Onan was given to Tamar to raise up a lineage for his deceased brother. He consented to the intercourse, but spilled his seed on the ground to keep from giving his brother a lineage. God was displeased with his wickedness and killed him also. Judah had a younger son which he promised to Tamar, but years went by and Tamar saw the promise was unfulfilled. In the meantime, Judah's wife died, and Tamar disguised herself as a prostitute to entice Judah to sleep with her. He did without knowing her identity, and she conceived. When it was discovered that she was pregnant, Judah determined to burn her for being with child "by whoredom." She then produced the pledges Judah had left with her for the sex, and the judgment was averted. Judah, unlike many practitioners of the double-standard, was honest enough to address the problem:

> And Judah acknowledged them, and said, *She hath been more righteous than I*; because that I gave her not to Shelah my son. And he knew her again no more. (Gen. 38:26)

A double-standard can be maintained for a short time, and men can take a very strong stand when it comes to the behavior of the women. Many men want loose women around and available—as long as they are not their own sisters and daughters. But Scripture tells us that sexual judgment will fall on the entire culture because of the immorality of the men, and this should also provide a motivation for masculine purity. Over time, men who patronize whores will watch their wives and daughters join the ranks of those whores—

> They sacrifice upon the tops of the mountains, and burn incense upon the hills, under oaks and poplars and elms, because the shadow thereof is good: *therefore your daughters shall commit whoredom, and your spouses shall commit adultery*. I will not punish your daughters when they commit whoredom, nor your spouses when they commit adultery: for themselves are separated with whores, and they sacrifice with harlots: therefore the people that doth not understand shall fall. (Hos. 4:13–14)

The headlines of our newspapers should remind us of our last motivation for pure living, and that is a prudent concern for good health—

And thou mourn at the last, *when thy flesh and thy body are consumed*, and say How have I hated instruction, and my heart despised reproof! (Prov. 5:11)

Sexually-transmitted diseases are God's way of chastizing sinful men. Catching some kind of creeping crud is therefore not a matter of chance; the universe is governed by a personal Lord who afflicts the immoral with the consequences of their behavior. A man with the clap is being visited by an angel of God, and he would do well to pay attention.

But having the motivation to avoid adultery is insufficient. We must also take care to attend to the *means* which the Bible assigns. The first thing a man should do is to *watch his doctrine*: "And by the fear of the Lord men depart from evil" (Prov. 16:6); "I have seen thine adulteries" (Jer. 13:27). God is present with every man in all that he does; a man cannot escape His omniscience. Contemplation of this truth is a wonderful damper to lust. It is hard to get going with the presence of the Lord at your left elbow.

A Christian man must also watch his own heart, and never begin to think that adultery is only located "out there" in the world, and has somehow been foisted upon him—"For out of the *heart* proceed . . . adulteries, fornications . . ." (Mt. 15:19). Peter begs *Christians* to abstain from fleshly lusts which war against the soul (1 Pet. 2:11). Paul tells Christians to put to death their members which are on the earth, and listed among those members are fornication and evil desire (Col. 3:5).

The overarching theme of this book has been to press upon men the duty a man has to love his wife. This also is a great sexual protection—and not just in the sense of providing godly motivation as discussed above. Paul teaches that because of sexual immorality, each man should have his own wife, and each woman have her own husband: "Let the husband render unto the wife due benevolence: and likewise also the wife unto the husband" (1 Cor. 7:2–3).

One of God's provisions against sexual temptation is good sex with a good woman. The expression that Paul uses here is filled with kindness. A wonderful session in bed is nothing but the exchange of benevolence. This could also lead to some interesting marital conversations—"Hey, baby, how about some due benevolence?"

A husband who wants to obey this commandment must watch his eyes: "Having *eyes* full of adultery . . . " (2 Pet. 2:14). As Job said, "I have made a covenant with mine *eyes*; why then should I think upon a maid?" (Job 31:1). When a man is watching his eyes, he is guarding more than just his thoughts. An attractive woman frequently knows when a man is looking her over, and consequently, if she wants to, has an opportunity to begin behaving in such a way as to reel him in. A man watching a woman sexually is more obvious than he usually thinks he is and consequently is more sexually vulnerable than he thinks he is.

An unmarried man can protect himself by listening to his parents:

> *My son, give me thine heart*, and let thine eyes observe my ways. For a whore is a deep ditch, and a strange woman is a narrow pit. She also lieth in wait as for a prey, and increaseth the transgressors among men. (Prov. 23:26–28)

And obviously, a man is protected from immorality through overall self-control:

> When I had fed them to the full, *they then committed adultery* and assembled themselves by troops in the harlots' houses. They were as fed horses in the morning: every one neighed after his neighbour's wife. (Jer. 5:7–8; cf. Ezek. 16:49)

The fact that they were stuffed with food was a contributor to their adulterous desire. The stomach was satisfied, time to move lower. By way of contrast, Paul teaches us the value of self-discipline in all things—"For I keep under my body and bring it into subjection: lest that by any means, when I have preached to others, I myself should be a castaway" (1 Cor. 9:27). This is especially important in resisting sexual tempation. Discipline in one area transfers to another, and lack of discipline in one area frequently overflows to others. A man should be self-disciplined in his work, his emotions, his recreations, and his appetites. If he is not, then he will have trouble staying in the right bed.

When a man has understood these biblical motivations, and has applied himself to the biblical means of avoiding adultery, he must still conduct himself with wisdom. This is because "adultery proper" is a very obvious sin, but the initial stirrings of it are *not* always so obvious. Compounding the problem, mistakes in judgment which set a man up for serious temptation are virtually invisible to all but the wise: "But strong meat belongeth to them that are of full age, even those who by reason of use have their senses exercised to discern both good and evil" (Heb. 5:14). Our senses do not need to be exercised very much in order to understand that standing around in the parking lot of the massage parlor is not a good idea. But we do need discernment in order to know how to avoid troublesome friendships, which may seem to us to be entirely innocent. Many snares wait for the unwary. Happily married men do not wake up one morning and decide they are going to commit adultery that day. Particularly with Christians, the consummation of infidelity usually comes as the last in a series of mild compromises and unobtrusive self-deceptions. More believing men have drifted into adultery than lurched into it.

This means that men must protect themselves from this sin when they do not feel like they need protection from it. This is because preparation is only possible when it is not *currently* necessary. A man in the grip of adulterous temptation is lying to others, and fundamentally to himself. This is why he should identify his standards long before he wants to lie to himself about the need for them. It is perhaps not surprising how frequently the Bible connects adultery with lying. This means that a man vulnerable to the temptation must study the truth long before the moment of crisis. In the moment of crisis he is not that interested in the truth. An innocent "friendship" can be resisted precisely because it is still (relatively) innocent. After the sexual element is manifest, the man doesn't want out. If he is wise, he should get out while he still doesn't want to—

> Behold, ye trust in *lying words*, that cannot profit. Will ye steal, murder, and *commit adultery*, and *swear falsely*, and burn incense unto Baal, and walk after other gods whom ye know not; and come and stand before me in this house, which is called by my name, and say, We are delivered to do all these abominations? Is this house, which is called by my name, become a den of robbers in your eyes? Behold, even I have seen it, saith the LORD. (Jer. 7:8–11)

Adulterous men are confused men; the confusion proceeds from lies, and advances on to more lies. The end result is that they are so blinded that they are willing to haul their adulteries into the Temple of God and say that they are delivered (by grace, no doubt) to "do all these abominations." The point is often repeated in Scripture—

> I have seen also in the prophets of Jerusalem an horrible thing: *they commit adultery, and walk in lies*: they strengthen also the hands of evildoers, that none doth return from his wickedness: they are all of them unto me as Sodom, and the inhabitants thereof as Gomorrah. (Jer. 23:14)

One of the more astonishing things about our modern immoralities is the identification we have sought to create between sexual laxity on the one hand and "openness and honesty" on the other. This is one of the central lies, which is the desire to detach lying as a way of life from adultery.

According to the drill, those who are faithful are repressed hypocrites, living a life of lies. The sexual libertine is frank, disarming, open, and all the rest of it. But the opposite is the case. Adulterers lie and faithful men tell the truth. However, because many men are quite sincere as they tell these lies, we therefore know that they must have been the very first to believe them. The first deception in this is usually self-deception—

> Because they have committed villany in Israel, and have *committed adultery* with their neighbours' wives, *and have spoken lying words* in my name, which I have not commanded them; even I know, and am a witness, saith the LORD. (Jer. 29:23)

Now this self-deceit has become common among evangelical Christians: "Thou that sayest a man should not commit adultery, dost thou commit adultery?" (Rom. 2:22). At the end of the road, the whole world can see the results of the scandal. Yet another pastor, counselor, or televangelist is caught *in flagrante*. But what did the deceit look like at the beginning? At the end, the "works of the flesh are *manifest*," and those works include adultery, fornication, uncleanness, and lasciviousness (Gal. 5:19). But what did they look like in their seed form?

Two aspects of this should be mentioned. The first is negative. Many of a man's sexual temptations begin with non-sexual temptations. When the author of Hebrews tells us to honor the marriage bed (Heb. 13:4), he immediately follows it up in the next verse with the charge to be *content* with what we have. A discontented man may chafe under any number of things. He may be unhappy with how his wife cooks, with how she disciplines the children, or with her weight. Or his discontent may have nothing directly to do with her—he may be unhappy with his boss, or with the amount of his paycheck. In any case, a discontented man is always sexually vulnerable. Another woman may represent a "way out" to him, or she may simply be a "reward" he gives himself for all the hard times he has to go through elsewhere. Discontent sets the snare, and sex is often the bait. Death is the trap.

Another area where men should guard themselves against adultery is in the area mentioned earlier of apparently innocent friendships. A man should resolve before God that he will have no one-on-one friendships (or close working relationships) with women unless they are with his mother, grandmother, sister, or wife. Now, what is meant by "friends"? We have been taught *ad nauseam* by means of feminist propaganda that men and women are simply interchangable units, and that we should work very hard to act as though this is so. The grand idea dictates that a man should be able to work with a woman and treat her like any of the other "guys" at work. If he and another guy could go out for lunch, why not have the same standard for a female co-worker? The answer, and I hate to belabor the obvious, is that under the clothes, their bodies are *different*, and hers looks like it would be a lot more fun than some male co-worker's body. In other words, one situation is sexually charged and the other one isn't. The man who believes all the current proganda on this subject is setting himself up for a dangerous fall.

A man who wants never to fall over a cliff should resolve never to tip-toe along the edge of it. This means that a man should always maintain an appropriate social distance between himself and any woman. This is not said to discourage friendships between couples, or the friendship of a couple with a woman who is single. It *is* meant to discourage the intimacy of friendship between one man and one woman when they are not bound together by covenant.

Now this standard is likely to be dismissed as legalism of some sort, so a word about the nature of these standards is necessary. This is an issue of wisdom, and not a question about the express law of God. Of course the Bible never says that a man cannot be alone with a women— think of our Lord with the woman at the well—and so this should be presented as a matter of discretion and wisdom. If the wounded man in the parable of the Good Samaritan had been a woman, we may still doubt that the Samaritan would have avoided her out of fear of scandal. Just to illustrate the principle, let us begin by granting every possible reasonable exception. Even so, wisdom still dictates that a man keep, as a matter of personal policy, a reasonable social distance from any woman who could conceivably be a sexual distraction or temptation. This would include one-on-one business lunches, giving rides, visiting at home when her husband is away, and so forth. Those who are serving in a pastoral or counseling role should take care that their ministry is in a public office, with people around, and a window in the door.

Now a man might protest that this kind of standard is unnecessary because his motives are pure. The first response to this is that he cannot know this in any absolute sense. The apostle Paul said his conscience was clear, but that this did not settle anything about it in any final sense: "For I know nothing by myself; yet am I not hereby justified: but he that judgeth me is the Lord" (1 Cor. 4:4). A man frequently does not know his own heart and motives until a wise man draws them out of him: "Counsel in the heart of man is like deep water; but a man of understanding will draw it out" (Prov. 20:5). Many men need to admit that there is far more "sex" in their "innocent" conversations than they might care to admit. If we take it a step beyond conversations to friendships, the danger increases.

A second response is that unless he has achieved perfection, he certainly goes through times when his motives are *not* pure: "For there is not a just man upon earth, that doeth good, and sinneth not" (Eccl. 7:20). The circumstances at one point in the relationship may be very different some months later. At one point, he was not tempted in the slightest degree. But later, when he is not walking with the Lord in the way he was earlier, his resolve is not what it was, and his situation *is* what it was—"For in many things we offend all" (Jas. 3:2). A man would be foolish indeed to say that he was impervious to all temptation of this nature. Many factors could be involved. His sexual relationship with his wife has deteriorated, or his woman friend has started wearing things she shouldn't, or a closer friendship develops than he has with his wife, and so on. A man who thinks he stands should take heed lest he fall (1 Cor. 10:12). He needs to be brutally honest with himself. Has he *never* looked at her walk across the room, or glanced at her breasts? If he has, then how can he deny the sexual element in the relationship?

A third protest to such a standard is that he can perhaps say honestly that his woman friend is not sexually attractive to him at all. "Look, if she were the last woman on earth . . ." But here he has forgotten to be a gentleman. Does he pose no problems of temptation for *her*? And that question cannot be answered by him unless he has gotten closer to her than he ought to be. He is caught in a bind. In sum, a man has no good reason for cultivating a close personal friendship with a woman who is not his wife or a close relative.

Supposed "professional" situations do not alter the principle. For example, suppose a man is a counselor or a pastor and women come to him seeking biblical direction and advice? He must never forget that his counsel is what a godly husband should be giving to this woman in the context of a covenantal sexual relationship. The street runs both ways, and a man who is not a husband who provides oversight and direction must labor to keep his distance. This is why Paul adds a telling comment for Timothy in his exhortation to him: "Rebuke not an elder, but intreat him as a father; and the younger men as brethren; the elder women as mothers; the younger as sisters, *with all purity*" (1 Tim. 5:1–2).

I have often said that a fully intimate relationship between a man and woman is like an unrolled carpet. Someone who wants to have a close and intimate relationship with a woman without sex is like someone who just wants to unroll the left side the carpet roll, while leaving the right side just the way it was. It is not going to happen that way. In many vocational situations (medicine, counseling, etc.), a man gets closer to a woman than he can safely be, and he finds himself tempted.

Finally, the avoidance of adultery is an expression of love—biblical love:

> Owe no man any thing, but to *love one another*: for he that loveth another hath fulfilled the law. For this, *Thou shalt not commit adultery*, Thou shalt not kill, Thou shalt not steal, Thou shalt not bear false witness, Thou shalt not covet; and if there be any other commandment, it is briefly comprehended in this saying, namely, Thou shalt love thy neighbour as thyself. Love worketh no ill to his neighbour: therefore love is the fulfilling of the law. (Rom. 13:8–10)

When a man fulfills the law of love—toward his wife through tender and sexual covenantal affection, and toward his neighbor and his neighbor's wife through his *lack* of sexual affection—then truly he works good to his family and no harm to his neighbor. In this he respects and honors *their* sexual affection. But a man who tolerates his lusts in the name of love is a declared enemy of every act of true benevolence that ever occurred in bed.

CHAPTER FIVE

Divorce

Divorce is not a legal issue with sexual consequences. In most cases it is a sexual issue with legal and covenantal consequences. And in the larger context, it is a sexual issue which results in something which God loathes (Mal. 2:16).

It is no coincidence that in the Sermon on the Mount, Christ teaches on divorce in the passage immediately following His instruction on lust. And although Christ taught in the section on lust that we should be willing to remove any member which stumbles us, He teaches in the portion on divorce that there is one member which is *not* to be removed. Put another way, a man should be more willing to multilate himself sexually than he is willing to put his wife away—

> Ye have heard that it was said by them of old time, Thou shalt not commit adultery: But I say unto you, That whosoever looketh on a woman to lust after her hath committed adultery with her already in his heart. And if thy right eye offend thee, pluck it out, and cast it from thee: for it is profitable for thee that one of thy members should perish, and not that thy whole body should be cast into hell. And if thy right hand offend thee, cut it off, and cast it from thee: for it is profitable for thee that one of thy members should perish, and not that thy whole body should be cast into hell. It hath been said, Whosoever shall put away his

wife, let him give her a writing of divorcement: But I say unto you, That whosoever shall put away his wife, saving for the cause of fornication, causeth her to commit adultery: and whosoever shall marry her that is divorced committeth adultery. (Mt. 5:27–32)

Most discussions about divorce get tangled up far too quickly in discussions of what is "legal." In others words, divorce is thought to be lawful if all the appropriate *t*'s are crossed and *i*'s are dotted. And in the words of the Westminster Confession, men are apt to "study arguments" in order to make sure the whole is legal. This can happen in both the civil and biblical realms. In other words, we often treat divorce in the text as a very wooden phenomenon. If it happened "this way," then it isn't adultery to remarry. If it happened the "other way," then it is. But our Lord teaches us here that divorce is a sexual phenomenon, and He relates it directly to a man's motivations. So while we do have to consider first the outline of the biblical teaching on the nature of divorce, we must not forget this motivational question, which we will return to at the end of our chapter.

Before we compare this section with Christ's teaching on divorce in Matthew 19, we see that we must first get the background of the teaching of the law as given by Moses:

When a man hath taken a wife, and married her, and it come to pass that she find no favour in his eyes, because he hath found some uncleanness in her: then let him write her a bill of divorcement, and give it in her hand, and send her out of his house. And when she is departed out of his house, she may go and be another man's wife. And if the latter husband hate her, and write her a bill of divorcement, and giveth it in her hand, and sendeth her out of his house; or if the latter husband die, which took her to be his wife; her former husband, which sent her away, may not take her again to be his wife, after that she is defiled; for that is abomination before the Lord: and thou shalt not cause the land to sin, which the Lord thy God giveth thee for an inheritance. (Deut. 24:1–4)

There are three basic truths which must be understood from this passage. First, divorce was limited by this law to certain specified causes. A man could not divorce his wife for trifling reasons; it had to be for "uncleanness." And, of course, given the general teaching of Mosaic law, this uncleanness could not just be *asserted*, it had to be established by at least two witnesses. Secondly, *if* he divorced his wife, a man also had to give his wife a bill of divorce. The process of divorce was thus made a formal judicial act. It would force men to think about the solemnity of what they were doing, and the legal ramifications of it. A man could not just tell his wife to get out, and then a few weeks later pretend that he had not done so. And third, a man who put away his wife could *not* have her back if she had married another man in the intervening time. In a very real sense, he was quite possibly burning his bridges. Putting her away meant the possibility of her remarriage, which meant that the law forbade any reconciliation after that point.

Now the Pharisees, *blinded by lust*, misunderstood all this. In His words, Christ attacks the distortions of the Pharisees, and not the teaching of Moses. This is clear from the encounter in Matthew 19:

> The Pharisees also came unto him, tempting him, and saying unto him, Is it lawful for a man to put away his wife *for every cause*? And he answered and said unto them, Have ye not read, that he which made them at the beginning made them male and female, And said, For this cause shall a man leave father and mother, and shall cleave to his wife: and they twain shall be one flesh? Wherefore they are no more twain, but one flesh. What therefore God hath joined together, let not man put asunder. They say unto him, Why did Moses then *command* to give a writing of divorcement, and to put her away? He saith unto them, Moses because of the hardness of your hearts suffered you to put away your wives: but from the beginning it was not so. And I say unto you, Whosoever shall put away his wife, except it be for fornication, and shall marry another, committeth

adultery: and whoso marrieth her which is put away doth commit adultery. (Mt. 19:3–9; cf. Mk. 10:1–12)

The Pharisees were saying that Moses *commanded* divorce, when he had done no such thing. Rather, he permitted and regulated it. Further, the question put to Christ was whether a man could put his wife away *for any reason.* Christ's answer was no. The lord of marriage is not the lusts of the husband. Consider for a moment what the phrase *for any reason* includes. They were maintaining that if a man found another woman with bigger breasts and longer legs, then God would approve when he ridded himself of his troublesome wife, the one with smaller breasts and short legs. In other words, these supposed "heirs" of Moses were using the words of Moses to recreate the very situation— easy divorce—which the law of Moses sought to restrain. When men advocate easy divorce "for any reason," a safe bet would be that lust for someone new is right at the heart of debate.

We now can consider the teaching of Christ. First, Christ teaches us that marriage is *not* absolute. The bond that unites a man and woman is *not* metaphysical; it is covenantal. This is very important. Under the law of God, marriage *can* be lawfully dissolved. But that dissolution had to do with *her* unfaithfulness. Unless he is putting her away for fornication, he is commiting adultery if he remarries, and he is tempting her to adultery, which she commits if *she* remarries. So the reasons for such dissolution are not to be found in the whims of men. "She burned the toast, and that very same day I met someone prettier." A man cannot avoid adultery in the sight of God just because he gets the right paperwork done. In other words, the Pharisees were trying to ground divorce in the lusts of the one initiating the divorcing. Christ grounded it in the law of God.

The ground that Christ mentions here is that of general sexual uncleanness—*porneias.* Of course what this means is that a man may divorce his wife because of her fornications. But more importantly, Christ bans all divorce that enables the man to gratify *his* lusts with other women. In other words, it is impossible to sanctify something that is essentially unclean.

Jesus was a teacher in Israel—and of course the children of Israel were the covenant people of God. They were in possession of the law of God, and marriages were ordinarily between covenant members. In this context, Christ taught plainly that the only grounds for dissolution of marriage was *porneias* on the part of the offending partner. Applied to our situation, the only ground for divorce between two professing Christians would be some kind of sexual infidelity on the part of one of them.

This brings us to the teaching of the apostle Paul on the subject of divorce. Jesus was teaching within the confines of the covenant nation of Israel. But when the gospel went out to the nations, the result of this great expansion was a huge increase in the number of *covenantally mixed marriages*. This had not been a problem before, and this new context gives us the interesting expression and teaching of Paul—*not I, but the Lord* and *I, not the Lord* (1 Cor. 7:10–16; 27–28). Paul and Christ are not at variance here; they are addressing different situations. But in every situation relating to divorce, it is important to remember the Lord's teaching and guard against legal excuses for lust.

In this new circumstance, the Corinthians had apparently asked Paul if they were in any way being spiritually defiled through sexual intercourse with pagan spouses. Given the nature of the situation, we may suppose that a few of the believers at Corinth were secretly hoping that the answer would be *yes*. But Paul answers that having sex with a pagan is not a problem. If the Corinthian believers were concerned that this would bring more pagan children in the world, Paul answers *no*. The children from such a union must be considered *saints* (1 Cor. 7:14).

But the pagan must be willing to live with the

Christian within the boundaries of marriage as biblically defined. Paul says that if the unbeliever is content or well-pleased to remain with the believer, then the believer must not divorce. The word he uses is *suneudokeo*, which means *to be pleased together with*. If the pagan is content with the arrangement, then the believer should not divorce. But if the unbeliever hits the road, then the believer is not bound in such circumstances and is certainly free to remarry— but only a Christian.

However, the real world is a messy place, and the number of variations on this can seem to a pastoral counselor almost interminable. Suppose a believer deserts a believer, with no *porneias* anywhere in sight? The one who left the marriage vows should be entreated by the church, and if there is no repentance, then church discipline should follow. This means that the one who deserted should now be treated as an unbeliever, which means that a divorce is permissible. But always remember that the point of all this is not to determine what is "legal," but rather to guard ourselves against what is lustful.

In many cases, it is necessary to reason biblically from the examples given in Scripture. This is because not every situation is covered, and we have to learn to think like Christians when it comes to situations that do not receive specific attention in the Bible. But reasoning from biblical case law *by analogy* is not a matter of making up law to suit yourself. For example, Jesus never addresses the subject of what to do with a man who is divorced by a woman. He talks about men divorcing wives, the wives so divorced, the women married by the men after such a divorce, the men who marry these divorced wives, and wives who divorce and marry another. But He never says anything about a man who is divorced by his wife. Is *he* free to remarry? In order to answer the question, we *have* to reason by analogy. If we refuse the legitimacy of reasoning by analogy, then we have to recognize that Jesus never addressed this situation directly. A man's wife divorced him, and if she ever marries, she is guilty of adultery (Mk. 10:12). But the Bible says nothing about that husband's status, meaning he is free to remarry. So reasoning from analogy and extention in such situations is absolutely necessary. Of course being married to an unbeliever frequently means that the couple do not share the same sexual ethic. We appear to have this situation in Ezra 9–10, where we are told that Israelite men were married to pagan women, who were guilty of "detestable practices." These were probably sexual in nature, and the response of Ezra is interesting. He *requires* the men to divorce their wives, and everything about the passage indicates that Ezra was in the right to do so. One of the ways we can see that we have taken in the secularist ethic surrounding us is that we think that Ezra overreacted, not realizing that relationships are more important than righteousness. But this is, of course, entirely false, and there are times when a Christian would be in sin for refusing to divorce a spouse.

This is just a brief outline of the basic biblical instruction on divorce, and should only be used to orient us; all the great problems are still not addressed. Or rather, put another way, *the* great problem is not addressed.

Most teaching on divorce should be directed where most of the problems are—right below the husband's belt buckle—"Whosoever putteth away his wife, and marrieth another, committeth adultery: and whosoever marrieth her that is put away from her husband committeth adultery" (Lk. 16:18). When Jesus teaches us that a look of lust amounts to adultery, He is saying that we cannot take refuge in the fact that we did not "do" anything about it, that everything stayed internal. In the same way, He says here that divorce cannot sanctify lust either. The fact that nothing was "done" does not justify the adulterer in his heart, and the fact that the adultery is "registered" at the county courthouse does not justify the adulterer who has paid all the appropriate attorney's fees. Unless it is made obvious, far too many Christians do not see the sexual element

whenever a man puts away his wife. The excuses and di-
versions may be many, but if hearts and minds were known,
the pleasing prospect of somebody new in bed is rarely far
away.

Of course this does not mean that a man can say his
behavior in divorcing his wife must therefore be legitimate
because "there was no lust involved." He would be far better off to take Christ at His word and doubt that he fully
understands the motives of his own heart.

A troubled marriage can be pretty tangled, and potential distractions abound. The problems can be financial, domestic, disciplinary, and so forth. But if the man is looking
to get out of the marriage, one basic assumption should be
that he would not mind making love to someone else. This
is not to deny the reality of these other problems or the
role they play in the disintegration of relationships. It is
simply to say that we must remember our Lord's teaching
on divorce, and where he placed that teaching. He brought
up the subject of divorce while He was discoursing on the
subject of lust.

The problem is obvious when a man leaves his wife for
another woman. But it is likely there when a man simply
leaves his wife for no one in particular. He is putting himself in position to find someone else, and he likes to be
able to point to all the "technical" and "legal" reasons why
he didn't ditch his wife for somebody else. Hypocrisy is a
real problem; it is perilously easy for a man to be a
hyprocrite in this way. He jumps to find "biblical grounds"
while inwardly relishing the thought of sex with someone
else. Perhaps he even believes his own lies. But the Lord
knows everything about the human heart, and we should
give Him credence in what He says at this point. The Lord
teaches on divorce in the context of lust, and we should
keep it there.

So a man intent on becoming a "one-woman man" must
see to it that he guards his heart in this area with all diligence. Jesus teaches us that divorce frequently ends with

adulterous unions. But we have neglected the corresponding truth that it frequently begins in adulterous intentions. Those intentions are frequently invisible to all except God—and those who ask to have them revealed.

CHAPTER SIX

Prostitution

Prostitution is the giving of sexual indulgence for hire or gifts. It is of course a kind of fornication or (if either of the parties is married) adultery. Consequently, many of the things addressed in other chapters will apply here as well. Despite the fact that this will be a short chapter, several factors peculiar to prostitution should nevertheless be mentioned here.

Harlotry is hardly the unforgiveable sin. Rahab was a harlot, servicing the men of a wicked city, and yet God brought her to faith: "Likewise also was not Rahab the harlot justified by works, when she had received the messengers, and had sent them out another way" (Jas. 2:25). This Rahab was brought into the covenant people of God and was privileged to be an ancestress of our Lord Jesus. Another woman in the Messiah's line was Tamar. She was greatly wronged by Judah, her father-in-law, and played the role of a harlot in order to lay claim on seed which was hers by law:

> And he turned unto her by the way, and said, Go to, I pray thee, let me come in unto thee; (for he knew not that she was his daughter in law.) And she said, What wilt thou give me, that thou mayest come in unto me? And he said, I will send thee a kid from the flock. And she said, Wilt thou give me a pledge, till thou send it? (Gen. 38:16–17)

When she was found to be pregnant, Judah resolved to have her burned, but she produced the securities he had given her, and he was forced to acknowledge her greater righteousness. (Incidentally, a case could be made here that Tamar did not sin at all. But that is a subject for another time.)

Harlotry is denounced clearly in Scripture, but, just as plainly, we are taught that there are other sins which place us much farther away from the kingdom of God: "Jesus saith unto them, Verily I say unto you, that the publicans and the harlots go into the kingdom of God before you. For John came unto you in the way of righteousness, and ye believed him not: but the publicans and the harlots believed him: and ye, when ye had seen it, repented not afterward, that ye might believe him" (Mt. 21:31–32). At the time of Christ, the hookers had a better shot at salvation than the well-respected theologians did.

But all this is to say that prostitution is a sin that is easier to repent of than pompous self-righteousness. It is *not* to say that it is not a very destructive sin. As I have given counsel to people caught in various sins, those involved in overt sexual sin are commonly very aware of their sinfulness. Those tangled up in doctrinal self-righteousness are often very far from the kingdom.

It is my intention to address two issues peculiar to prostitution here. The first is that the rationalization that can occur when men resort to prostitutes is very different than the rationalization that occurs when they are sleeping with their fiancees. The reason he is sleeping with his fiancee (he says) is that they are so deeply committed to one another. They are in love, his thinking goes, and as countless rock songs have expressed this view, how can it be wrong when it feels so right? The sex is justified because this person means *everything* to the man. Fornicaton is often justified by an appeal to romanticism.

But the use of prostitutes is often rationalized in the opposite way. In other words, it is not wrong because it doesn't mean *anything*. She was working the brothel that night; she was going to be having sex with somebody; the two of them have no relationship whatever. The "relationship" is meaningless, and so therefore no one should be upset over the meaning of it. The use of a prostitute is justified by means of a reductionism. But the meaning of the sexual union is what God says it is, and not what our emotions say about it. When Paul told the Christian men in the church at Corinth to stop frequenting sacred prostitutes, he did not consult their feelings. A sexual union creates a one-flesh bond (1 Cor. 6:15–16), whether or not the man feels like anything happened. He says, "It is nothing." God says something else. He says that she was just a piece of meat that he used to get off. This is quite true of his emotional frame of mind, and because she is *not* just a piece of meat, but is created in the image of God, his emotional attitude, far from justifying him, condemns him further.

The other aspect of prostitution should be obvious. Men who do not have sexual self-control, and who use prostitutes, are going to wind up spending a lot of money. Like the son in the story Christ told, they waste their substance on a series of sexual experiences—"Whoso loveth wisdom rejoiceth his father: but he that keepeth company with harlots spendeth his substance" (Prov. 29:3). Put another way, a frequenter of prostitutes is a sexual spendthrift.

All sexual experiences have economic consequences. Within the bonds of marriage, the man and the woman are both blessed. When a man spends his substance on whores, he tears himself down. Prostitution is not what a man's lusts describe it as being. Men who do not think through the issues carefully can be easily led astray here. The experience can be made very pleasant indeed. But the end, as Scripture declares, is death.

CHAPTER SEVEN

Rape

The subject of this chapter might seem at first glance to be an *odd* inclusion, but careful consideration should reveal that teaching is needed here as much as in any other sexual area. We live in a time when our language has been much debased for political and ideological reasons, and we must always take care to define sin biblically. Radical feminists have charged that any heterosexual intercourse falls under the heading of rape and is therefore intolerable and oppressive. If Christians do not study what the Bible teaches, the tendency will be to be affected by such unbiblical assumptions and definitions, and then to drift into them. That process of drifting will be invisible to those who have succumbed to it, and in our day it is already occurring within the church.

One of the first things we must do in seeking to understand this is to take a stand against the sexual relativism of those who are most shrill about the evil of rape. If we do not have the standards of the Bible, then the only way we can make judgments about the sexual behavior of anyone is on the basis of personal preference. In other words, if God will not judge the rapist on the Last Day, then all the feminist screeds in the world should not make a rapist feel bad about what he is doing. A great desire is evident in our culture to "absolutize" the evil of rape, but since the process is an arbitrary one, suspended in midair, there is no reason to take it seriously. In a world without absolutes grounded in the character of *God*, a man can take what he wants. And if what he wants is an otherwise unattainable woman, then rape is a live option. So the only way to condemn any rape is to turn to the standards of God's law. But once we have done this, we discover that *some* situations which our society calls rape should not be included.

Violent rape is a judgment of God upon a people: "For I will gather all nations against Jerusalem to battle; and the city shall be taken, and the houses rifled, *and the women ravished*; and half of the city shall go forth into captivity, and the residue of the people shall not be cut off from the city" (Zech. 14:2). This does not justify the perpetrators; it is simply the recognition that when disaster befalls a city, sexual disaster for the women is part of this. This does not mean that a woman who is raped should assume any personal responsibility for it; she is innocent. In his great work, *The City of God*, St. Augustine was correct to lament the Christian virgins who had committed suicide rather than face rape from the invading barbarians. This was not necessary. Violent rape is God's judgment upon a culture, and individual women who are part of that culture are included in the judgment. But this does not mean that they as individuals "deserved" it.

Job recognized this judgment aspect of rape: "If mine heart have been deceived by a woman, or if I have laid wait at my neighbour's door; then let my wife grind unto another, and let others bow down upon her" (Job 31:9). "Grinding wheat" is an obvious sexual metaphor. Job is saying that if he has behaved in an unlawful way, then he is willing to invite the judgment of God upon his household. That judgment would include his wife "grinding unto another."

We see the same judgment at work in disintegrating cultures: "Because sentence against an evil work is not executed speedily, therefore the heart of the sons of men is fully set in them to do evil" (Eccl. 8:11). Here the rape is not being perpetrated by foreign soldiers, but is the result of citizens turning on one another. Every culture is a gathering of sinners, and so rape is always a possibility. But when God's hand of judgment is heavy upon a people, women are in far greater danger of sexual assault than at other times. It is interesting to note that in these, our "enlightened" times, a woman is far more likely to be abused in this way than before all the liberation happened.

When a man has intercourse with a woman contrary to the laws of marriage, and she is unwilling, a rape has been committed. When this is done criminally, violently, the biblical penalty varies according to the marital state of the woman—

> But if a man find a betrothed damsel in the field, and the man force her, and lie with her: then the man only that lay with her shall die: but unto the damsel thou shalt do nothing; there is in the damsel no sin worthy of death: for as when a man riseth against his neighbour, and slayeth him, even so is this matter: for he found her in the field, and the betrothed damsel cried, and there was none to save her. If a man find a damsel that is a virgin, which is not betrothed, and lay hold on her, and lie with her, and they be found; then the man that lay with her shall give unto the damsel's father fifty shekels of silver, and she shall be his wife; because he hath humbled her, he may not put her away all his days. (Deut. 22:25–29)

A married or betrothed woman is protected by her husband, even if he is not present to protect her. If she is a married woman, the penalty for rape is death for the rapist. We see in this passage, the recognition that rape is comparable to murder. A woman might be raped, contrary to her will, in just the way that a man might be murdered contrary to his will. In this we see that there is no basis for punishing or ostracizing the woman.

If the woman is not married or betrothed, the penalty is different. The rapist is compelled to pay the bride price (which restored her position in society), can be forced to marry her, and does not have the option of divorcing her. Now this does not mean that the woman was forced into a marriage with the man who raped her. We see elsewhere in cases of seduction, that a father could refuse to give his daughter away in marriage, and we can see how the situation would be the same here (Exod. 22:16–17). Rapists are hardly a good pool for selecting fine sons-in-law. So if the father refused to give his daughter in marriage, the bride price would still have to be paid, and the rapist would be forced to restore (as much as possible) the woman's marriagability.

Modern critics of course point to this discrepancy of punishment as an example of how the Bible treats women as chattel, a commodity that men trade in all patriarchal societies. Nothing could be farther from the reality. When a married or betrothed woman is raped, there is no possibility of any kind of restitution, and so the full force of the penalty falls upon the man, and the penalty is death. When a woman is unattached, the rapist is forced to restore her marriagibility, either by marrying her himself, or by providing her with a bride price. Compare this to what happens to a rapist in our society, and what happens to the women, and we see the immediate discrepancy. Biblical law is far more concerned for the sexual protection of women than is our culture, despite our empassioned rhetoric on the point.

The situation with Jacob's daughter Dinah was probably similar to this latter situation. The text says that "when Shechem the son of Hamor the Hivite, prince of the country, saw her, he took her, and lay with her, and defiled her" (Gen. 34:2). But it also says that the young man loved her *after* the rape, unlike Amnon with Tamar, and "his soul clave unto Dinah the daughter of Jacob, and he loved the damsel, and spake kindly unto the damsel" (v. 3). The fact that such comfort was needed indicates that this was in fact a rape. But we are told later that this young man was "more honourable than all the house of his father" (v. 19). He had raped her but then sought marriage and was willing to pay any retroactive dowry or gift (v. 12). Simeon and Levi required that their entire people be circumcised, and when they had done so, the brothers attacked them with the sword. Jacob was greatly displeased with their behavior. They had made him odious to the surrounding people, and the worst thing about it is that they had made the covenant sign of circumcision into a weapon of war. Their violence is the reason a blessing passed them by. Instruments of cruelty were in their habitations (Gen. 49:5).

Our civil law includes the category of statutory rape, which is certainly a biblical concept. If someone under the age of adult responsibility is forcibly taken away (whether for sexual purposes or not), the crime is a species of kidnapping, which in Scripture deserves the death penalty. Part of the reason why a society should have wise and godly men for judges is that they must determine in such cases whether the one raped is almost of age. But when we are dealing with young children who are abused by adults (pederasty, child porn, etc.) the penalty for those guilty of the crime should be death.

The distance between a biblical culture and a pagan one is seen in the treatment of women who were taken captive in war. Although rape is very common in war, God did not permit it in the armies that represented His holiness:

> When thou goest forth to war against thine enemies, and the LORD thy God hath delivered them into thine hands, and thou hast taken them captive, and seest among the captives a beautiful woman, and hast a desire unto her, that thou wouldest have her to thy wife; then thou shalt bring her home to thine house; and she shall shave her head, and pare her nails; and she shall put the raiment of her captivity from off her, and shall remain in thine house, and bewail her father and her mother a full month: and after that thou shalt go in unto her, and be her husband, and she shall be thy wife. And it shall be, if thou have no delight in her, then thou shalt let her go whither she will;

but thou shalt not sell her at all for money, thou shalt not make merchandise of her, because thou hast humbled her. (Deut. 21:10–14)

The required biblical treatment of a captive woman here is remarkable for the humanity it displays. Although a modern feminist would consider this a complicated form of rape, the legal protections for women—even women from alien, unbelieving cultures—are considerable. An Israelite man could not take a woman in the lustful aftermath of battle, he could not have what he wanted "right now," and he had to respect her duty to mourn for her family. After a month had passed, he could marry her, but her status was therefore elevated to that of a true wife. If she were used sexually, she could not be sold as a slave. She was a wife, and if divorced, she had to be dismissed as a wife. When biblical law is read thoughtfully and carefully, it is plain that a wall of protection is built around women, and many restrictions are placed upon the men.

A final aspect of rape that should be briefly mentioned is perhaps closer to home. Because we have forgotten the biblical concepts of true authority and submission, or more accurately, have rebelled against them, we have created a climate in which caricatures of authority and submission intrude upon our lives with violence.

When we quarrel with the way the world *is*, we find that the world has ways of getting back at us. In other words, however we try, the sexual act cannot be made into an egalitarian pleasuring party. A man penetrates, conquers, colonizes, plants. A woman receives, surrenders, accepts. This is of course offensive to all egalitarians, and so our culture has rebelled against the concept of authority and submission in marriage. This means that we have sought to suppress the concepts of authority and submission as they relate to the marriage bed.

But we cannot make gravity disappear just because we dislike it, and in the same way we find that our banished authority and submission comes back to us in pathological forms. This is what lies behind sexual "bondage and sub-mission games," along with very common rape fantasies. Men dream of being rapists, and women find themselves wistfully reading novels in which someone ravishes the "soon to be made willing" heroine. Those who deny they have any need for water at all will soon find themselves lusting after polluted water, but water nonetheless.

True authority and true submission are therefore *an erotic necessity*. When authority is honored according to the word of God it serves and protects—and gives enor-mous pleasure. When it is denied, the result is not "no authority," but an authority which devours.

CHAPTER EIGHT

Polygamy

Like the last chapter, this one may appear at first glance to be an odd inclusion in a modern book on sexual fidelity. Polygamy is not a rampant problem in the modern church. *Yet*.

We live in a time of sexual chaos and relativism. The older monogamous order was most certainly a Christian order, and we will soon discover that the one cannot be maintained apart from the other. Just as this Christian order is under assault with reference to its stern prohibitions of fornication, adultery, and sodomy, we cannot expect other elements of our Christian marital heritage to remain.

Homosexual activists are currently conducting a full-court press against the Christian definition of marriage; homosexuals want to be able to marry, adopt children, and so forth. When that definition falls (as it appears it soon will), then we have no foundation in our law against the practice of polygamy either. Who are we to restrict the choices of others? When we have abandoned in our law any transcendent reason for defining marriage as we do, the immediate result will be the necessary definition of marriage according to the practices and desires of men. And one of those desires will be to bed down a lot of women, along with paperwork to make it respectable.

Among more conservative Christians, the immediate problem will *not* be the toleration of sodomy. The problem will arise when an evangelical church is approached with a request for membership by a man with three wives. His three wives will be perfectly legal according to the new "who's-to-say-what-marriage-is" laws, and he wants to know why he is being refused membership. *Abraham* had multiple wives. Would he, the father of all the faithful, be excluded from membership too? It would be kind of ironic, he muses, if Abraham could not be a member of the church, which is really nothing more than the society of the sons of Abraham.

Sadly, our churches exclude polygamy now, not because we have developed the scriptural case against it, but rather because we are enjoying the vestiges of the old order. Polygamy is still against the law, and so our churches do not have to deal with it. But the old order is wobbly, and the church needs to think through the options when the civil definition of marriage becomes radically unbiblical. Some might object that it is not that simple and never is. But one thing is certain—churches had better think through this issue before it becomes a pressing pastoral problem. This chapter is simply a suggested starting point in the discussion.

We should start by understanding that monogamy is required by the creation norm. We do not find polygamy in the Garden of Eden; the first mention of it comes with the ungodly Lamech: "And Lamech took unto him two wives: the name of the one was Adah, and the name of the other Zillah" (Gen. 4:19). When God created Adam, He says something unique in the creation narrative. Elsewhere God has been proclaiming that His work of creation was "very good." But after Adam was made, God said that it was "not good" that the man should be alone (Gen. 2:18). In this particular case, *not good* meant *not done*. Had the creation of Adam completed the creation of mankind, God would have pronounced the blessing of "very good," as He had done with everything else. But Adam alone was only half of mankind—"So God created man in his own image, in the image of God created he him; male and female created he them" (Gen. 1:27). The Bible is plain that God created *man* both male and female.

God assigned to Adam the task of naming all the animals, and Adam found that among the animals no helper could be considered suitable for him (2:20):

> And the LORD God caused a deep sleep to fall upon Adam, and he slept: and he took one of his ribs, and closed up the flesh instead thereof; and the rib, which the LORD God had taken from man, made he a woman, and brought her unto the man. And Adam said, This is now bone of my bones, and flesh of my flesh: she shall be called Woman, because she was taken out of Man. (Gen. 2:21–23)

The first point to note is that when God determined to solve the problem of Adam's loneliness, He did not do it with a harem. He created one man and then one woman. He did not create Adam and Eve, followed closely by Suzy, Sally, and Henrietta.

The text sees this creation order *as normative for all time.* A lesson is drawn from this for all Adam's sons who take a wife. Adam, who had no human father or mother, is nevertheless the pattern for all men who leave their fathers and mothers. Because Adam took Eve, all men descended from him should leave their fathers and mothers. Adam was created, not just as an individual, but also as a pattern for all men—

> Therefore shall a man leave his father and his mother, and shall cleave unto his wife: and they shall be one flesh. And they were both naked, the man and his wife, and were not ashamed. (Gen. 2:24–25)

This pattern is plain. From this we may conclude that Adam and Eve were created, male and female, to model for us the way God intends for us to live. This creation pattern therefore excludes both sexual perversities like sodomy and bestiality, and sexual curiosities like polygamy.

Homosexuality is excluded because God did not create another man for Adam. Bestiality is excluded because no helper was found for Adam among the animals. And as we discussed in the previous chapter, our Lord taught that in this passage divorce is excluded as well: "And he answered and said unto them, Have ye not read, that he which made them *at the beginning* made them male and female" (Mt. 19:4).

Any argument from Genesis which excludes divorce will also necessarily exclude polygamy *on the same principle*. Jesus was arguing that God created one man and one woman, which meant that the one man was not supposed to leave her for another one. But the reasoning which excludes taking women serially also prohibits taking them in tandem. The reason for this is that God created *two*; marriages which involve more than two are not consistent with God's creation design.

We also see this pattern in God's redemptive design as well. The Lord Jesus Christ is a monogamist. He is the bridegroom and there is only one bride: "And I John saw the holy city, new Jerusalem, coming down from God out of heaven, prepared as a bride adorned for her husband" (Rev. 21:2). This holy city is the Church, the bride of Christ. Now the very idea of Christ as polygamist is an obnoxious one. A central part of the victory of Christ was the establishment of unity, unity throughout heaven and earth. There is one Lord, one faith, one baptism.

Now, armed with this example, Christian men are told to cultivate the same kind of love for their wives—

> For the husband is the head of the wife, even as Christ is the head of the church: and he is the saviour of the body. . . . Husbands, love your wives, even as Christ also loved the church, and gave himself for it. (Eph. 5:23, 25)

A man cannot imitate Christ by pursuing more than one woman. A Christ-like love is necessarily a monogamous love. That is why this pattern for Christian marriage is to be reflected in the eldership of the church. Paul insists that a "bishop then must be blameless, *the husband of one wife*" (1 Tim. 3:2). He says the same thing to Titus, as he is establishing churches in Crete:

> For this cause left I thee in Crete, that thou shouldest set in order the things that are wanting, and ordain elders in every city, as I had appointed thee: If any be blameless, *the husband of one wife*, having faithful children not accused of riot or unruly. For a bishop must be blameless. (Tit. 1:5–7)

The Bible flatly excludes polygamists from the leadership of the church. This means that, over time, as the gospel takes root in any given culture, polygamy will be excluded there as well. Polygamous societies generally encourage the taking of multiple wives as an indication of wealth or status—the man most likely to be in leadership in that society was also most likely to have more than one wife. But to the extent that the gospel influences that society, such men are relegated to the back pews. They are told that what they previously thought of as a sign of their ability to lead is actually their most obvious *disqualification* for leadership.

We may conclude, from God's creation design, from God's redemptive design, and from the specific instructions of the New Testament for Christian leaders, that polygamy falls plainly short of God's standards for marital behavior. Put another way, the Christian faith is necessarily monogamous.

But having said all this, we must be careful to exclude polygamy in the same way in which Scripture does. If polygamy were to become legal, and a man were to take more than one wife, and he then came to Christ, divorce would not be an option for him. The same thing goes for those societies where polygamy is still an aspect of their culture—this is a very real problem for missionaries. The polygamist and all his wives, if they profess faith, should be received into the membership of the church. He should continue to live with them as wives, including an ongoing sexual relationship with all of them. But this is only safe to do if the church is clear on the *absolute necessity* of setting a monogamous example in the leadership of the church.

If the wives in question are true wives, then the church should recognize that fact. To go beyond this is to legislate contrary to Scripture. The passages which describe polygamy *are* in the Bible, and refusing to answer the arguments of the coming polygamists will do no good at all—"And David dwelt with Achish at Gath, he and his men, every man with his household, even David with his two wives, Ahinoam the Jezreelitess, and Abigail the Carmelitess, Nabal's wife" (1 Sam. 27:3). A little later, it says, "And David took him more concubines and wives out of Jerusalem, after he was come from Hebron: and there were yet sons and daughters born to David" (2 Sam. 5:13).

Polygamy cannot be considered a sin in the same way that adultery is. It does fall short of the creation pattern, but it is a sin which can be culturally tolerated until the leaven of the gospel causes it naturally to disappear. We can see the contrast between adultery and polygamy in the exchange between Nathan and David, when Nathan came to rebuke him for his *adultery*:

> And Nathan said to David, Thou art the man. Thus saith the LORD God of Israel, I anointed thee king over Israel, and I delivered thee out of the hand of Saul; And *I gave thee* thy master's house, and *thy master's wives* into thy bosom, and gave thee the house of Israel and of Judah; and if that had been too little, I would moreover have given unto thee such and such things. (2 Sam. 12:7–8)

When the church faces all that Scripture teaches on this subject, it will have a strong position indeed. God forbids polygamy in the ordinances of creation and redemption, but polygamy may be tolerated only among those *not* suitable for leadership in the church. If those not qualified for leadership in the church are allowed undisputed possession of the biblical passages which describe and tolerate polygamy, then the church will not be in a position to answer responsibly. The church can never answer responsibily with only a *portion* of the Bible. Put simply, this means that the church should forbid leadership to polygamists and reluctantly tolerate membership for polygamists.

At the same time, in addition to the doctrinal grounds discussed earlier, the teaching of the church should absolutely discourage the practice of polygamy by anyone within the church on the basis of its unbiblical nature and practical folly. In other words, if a married man who is already a member of the church begins to think about taking another wife, and the church has already clearly declared the teaching of the Bible on this, then that man is sinning against greater light, and could come under the discipline of the church. A man who comes to the church as a polygamist should be received, but with clear teaching that he is not to add any more wives. A man who seeks to become a polygamist while already a member of the church should be rebuked and censured.

We have already considered the unbiblical character of polygamy. But what can we say from Scripture on the lack of wisdom displayed in it? First, polygamy sets up a situation in which destructive competition between wives is hardly possible to avoid—"And he went in also unto Rachel, and *he loved also Rachel more than Leah*, and served with him yet seven other years" (Gen. 29:30). This was a horrible situation which soon involved two wives, two handmaids, and the great baby race.

The likelihood of this kind of problem can be seen in the fact that biblical law had to address it with particular legislation—

> If a man have two wives, one *beloved*, and another *hated*, and they have born him children, both the beloved and the hated; and if the firstborn son be hers that was hated: Then it shall be, when he maketh his sons to inherit that

which he hath, that he may not make the son of the beloved firstborn before the son of the hated, which is indeed the firstborn: But he shall acknowledge the son of
the hated for the firstborn, by giving him a double portion
of all that he hath: for he is the beginning of his strength;
the right of the firstborn is his. (Deut. 21:15–17)

Polygamy breeds competition and envy among wives.
This is why the law forbids a man from introducing this
kind of tense relationship between sisters—"Neither shalt
thou take a wife to her sister, to vex her, to uncover her
nakedness, beside the other in her life time" (Lev. 18:18).
Notice the language; to take a woman's sister as a second
wife would be to *vex* her. The vexation could be the result
of simple old-fashioned jealousy, but it could also be related to the very natural tendency to favor one wife over
the other in very practical ways. We noted above the restriction on favoring the children of a loved wife, but the
Bible also addresses the day-to-day problems: "And if he
have betrothed her unto his son, he shall deal with her after the manner of daughters. If he take him another wife;
her food, her raiment, and her duty of marriage, shall he
not diminish" (Exod. 21:9–10). Under the law a man was
permitted to take a second wife, but the practice was
bounded in various ways. One of the boundaries was that a
man was not permitted to diminish the marital rights of his
first wife. Those marital rights included her food, her cloth-
ing, and her right to him sexually. Why this law? Clearly it
is because sinful men would be likely to practice "divorce
and remarriage" under the cover of polygamy. They could
leave a wife while letting her stay in the house, and bring in
a second wife. This was flatly prohibited.

Secondly, if polygamy were a positive good, then there
would be no reason for the Bible to restrict it, as even the
Old Testament does, for kings and rulers: "Neither shall
he multiply wives to himself, that his heart turn not away:
neither shall he greatly multiply to himself silver and gold
(Deut. 17:17). This law was overtly disobeyed by Solomon,

and the promised judgment fell on him: "And he had seven hundred wives, princesses, and three hundred concubines: and *his wives turned away his heart*" (1 Kgs. 11:3). The Bible does not consider polygamy a prerogative of royalty; the king was the one person in Israel who was prohibited from being one who multiplied wives, and he was the one who was most likely to be in a position to do so.

Now the prohibition is on the multiplication of wives (clearly the fault of Solomon). It could be argued that the law did not expressly prohibit a king like David from *adding* wives, which is likely, given how Nathan spoke to David after his sin with Bathsheba. A king was forbidden to multiply wives, and yet Nathan told David that God would have given him other wives instead of Bathsheba (2 Sam. 12:8).

But this brings us to the third and last consideration of the practical folly inherent in polygamy. When a man is polygamous, it puts him in a position where he can father more children than he can be a father to. Even a "mild" polygamist like David could father many more children than he could possibly be a father to. And this is evident in the course of David's history with his children. One of his sons, Amnon, raped one of his daughters, Tamar, and another one of his sons, Absalom, took his own vengeance by killing Amnon after David did nothing about it but get angry. The end result of all this was a civil war between David and Absalom, a war which David did not want to fight and reluctantly won.

When David sinned with Bathsheba, God had promised that certain consequences would follow—"Thus saith the LORD, Behold, I will raise up evil against thee out of thine own house, and I will take thy wives before thine eyes, and give them unto thy neighbour, and he shall lie with thy wives in the sight of this sun" (2 Sam. 12:11). This melancholy prophecy was fulfilled by David's own son. He slept with his father's wives on the roof of the palace, in the sight of all Israel. And thus the progeny of

David's polygamy insulted both him and his wives, and showed how polygamy is not filled with life and peace but leads only to vicious ambition and lust.

Polygamy, in all its aspects, is covenantal fruitlessness.

CHAPTER NINE

Sodomy

Within the last generation we have seen a remarkable cultural transition, a transition in which the once-common rejection of homosexual behavior has been itself rejected. Prior to this transition, not only was homosexuality disapproved socially, it was also, in most places, against the law.

As Christians, we must be willing to hold everything up against the standard of Scripture. Is this new cultural development an example of refreshing biblical tolerance? Or is it a case of sexual apostasy?

In examining the direction our culture has taken on this issue, a good place to start would be in distinguishing sins from crimes. A sin is something which is to be rejected on moral grounds; a crime is a particular behavior to which a civil penalty ought to be attached. The two categories of course overlap, but not completely. Something can be sinful, like covetousness, and yet not be criminal behavior. And a sin like murder both a sin and a crime. Our first consideration should therefore be whether or not the Bible teaches that homosexuality is a sin, and then, if so, whether or not it should also be prohibited under the law. Should homosexuality be treated as criminal conduct?

So is it sin? Our first appeal in sexual matters should always be to the creation order. As we have already seen, when the Lord Jesus taught on divorce, He appealed to God's "original intent" at the creation. Subsequent law about divorce took the hard realities of sin and rebellion into account, but those who wanted to know *what marriage was intended to be* were told to look at how it was from the beginning. God created one man, one woman, one time. God created Adam, and after Adam had named the beasts it was apparent there was no helper suitable for him among those animals (Gen. 2:18). God then put Adam into a deep sleep, and from Adam's body, He fashioned Eve.

Because of this creation order, we can see any number of sexual combinations excluded—polygamy, bestiality, serial polygamy through divorce, and pertinent to our subject here, homosexuality. God created *Eve* for Adam, and not another man.

Consequently, given this creation order, we should not be surprised that God flatly prohibits homosexuality throughout the rest of Scripture. For example, in Romans the apostle Paul says this:

> Wherefore God also gave them up to uncleanness through the lusts of their own hearts, to dishonour their own bodies between themselves: who changed the truth of God into a lie, and worshipped and served the creature more than the Creator, who is blessed for ever. Amen. For this cause God gave them up unto vile affections: for even their women did change the natural use into that which is against nature: And likewise also the men, leaving the natural use of the woman, burned in their lust one toward another; men with men working that which is unseemly, and receiving in themselves that recompence of their error which was meet. (Rom. 1:24–27)

In this place, the desire for sexual gratification from a member of one's own sex is described as a dishonorable and "vile affection," one which is "unseemly," and heterosexual intercourse is described as "the natural use of the woman." Lesbianism is described as being "against nature." The behavior is described as self-destructive because those who burn with lust in this way receive in themselves a natural penalty.

Eternal consequences follow such behavior as well: "Know ye not that the unrighteous shall not inherit the kingdom of God? Be not deceived: neither fornicators, nor idolaters, nor adulterers, nor *effeminate*, nor *abusers of themselves with mankind*, nor thieves, nor covetous, nor drunkards, nor revilers, nor extortioners, shall inherit the kingdom of God. And such were some of you: but ye are washed, but ye are sanctified, but ye are justified in the name of the Lord Jesus, and by the Spirit of our God" (1 Cor. 6:9–11). This passage is important for a number of reasons. First, when we consider how homosexuality is listed here, it gives the lie to the common accusation of "homophobia." Paul rejects homosexuality firmly, but does not treat it any differently than any other of a number of sins, both heterosexual sins and nonsexual sins. Homosexuality is condemned in a list which includes adultery and fornication, along with covetousness and drunkenness.

Further, the condemnation of homosexual behavior is very clear indeed. The word translated "effeminate" is *malakos* and refers to the male who plays the female in homosexual intercourse. This partner is the passive partner, i.e., a catamite. The "abuser of himself with mankind" is a translation of *arsenokoites*, meaning one who lies with a male as with a female. Apart from the repentance and faith, the catamite receives, and the sodomite gives, not a kinky time in bed, but rather damnation. But Paul takes it for granted that such can be forgiven and cleansed. He tells the Corinthian church that "such were some of you."

The Old Testament is just as clear on this subject as the New, and the language is blunt:

> There shall be no whore of the daughters of Israel, nor a sodomite of the sons of Israel. Thou shalt not bring the hire of a whore, or the price of a dog, into the house of the Lord thy God for any vow: for even both these are abomination unto the Lord thy God. (Deut. 23:17–18)

This is not just a rejection of sodomy, but also a contemptuous rejection of it. The price of a sodomite is described as the price of a dog. This is the probable reason for the apostle John's exclusion of "dogs" from the New Jerusalem, which is to be understood as the Christian Church— "For without are dogs, and sorcerers, and whoremongers, and murderers, and idolaters, and whosoever loveth and maketh a lie" (Rev. 22:15).

This passage also makes plain that our deeply-felt desire to separate homosexuality from the worship of the God of the Bible is the result of us having learned what the Bible teaches. It is not something we gathered from natural law. In this passage from Deuteronomy, we see that the Israelites had to be instructed that a prostitute's wage-earnings should not be accepted as a gift to the Lord. In the same way, a man who earned money through sodomite prostitution was prohibited from giving any of the proceeds to the Lord as well.

When Israel fell away from the teaching of God's law, this important separation of worship and sodomy was lost. Speaking of the reforms of Josiah, the Biblical writer says this: "And he brake down the houses of the sodomites, that were by the house of the Lord, where the women wove hangings for the grove" (2 Kgs. 23:7).

We can readily see that the Bible defines homosexuality as a sin, but it acknowledges that the sin is one which some might want to bring into the worship of God. That kind of compromise is flatly prohibited. Those who live in this way, as Paul reminded us, will not inherit the kingdom of heaven.

But we must be careful. Before proceeding further, we need to take a short detour to consider how a biblical understanding of sin in general is necessary as we work our way though our treatment of this sin in particular. A common assumption among many is that ability limits ethical obligation. We tend to define sin by whether or not we could have avoided it. If something is unavoidable, then we assume that no moral culpability can be assigned to it.

This premise, which many share both inside and outside the church, is the reason why researchers are so interested in finding a homosexual "gene." It also explains why the media reports on any progress in that research with such great shouts of gladness and joy. If it can only be shown that someone was *born* a homosexual, then we certainly cannot blame him for it.

In contrast, a biblical understanding of sin is that it must be defined according to the standards of the Word of God. We must maintain this for two reasons. First, the Bible defines sin in this way, without any reference to human inability. For example, the apostle John defines sin as *lawlessness* (1 Jn. 3:4). Sin is defined by what the law of God says we must do or not do and not by what we say we think we are able to do.

Secondly, the Bible acknowledges freely that sinful men do not have the ability to do what is right. Prior to the coming of the grace of God, we were slaves to sin (Rom. 6:17). A slave is one who is in bondage. So sin is not defined by human inability, but rather by the law of God. The search for a homosexual gene must therefore be considered irrelevant. We already know that *heterosexual* sins have a genetic foundation, but this does not excuse the sin. This is because sin is not defined by the nature of man, but rather by what is contrary to the nature and character of God.

Understanding this is very important for a Christian man who struggles with homosexual temptation. The first step in deliverance is understanding how inflexible the law of God is at this point. There is *no* deliverance in reinterpretation, or softening the standard. Grasping the teaching of the Word on the nature of bondage to sin is also important in order to prevent a desire for "quick fixes." Paul does tell the Corinthians that "such were some of you," clearly showing that a man can be an ex-homosexual. Forgiveness and deliverance through the Gospel is available to all kinds of men, including all kinds of homosexuals.

Having said this, we still have to acknowledge that there are different kinds of homosexuals, and the Scripture offers different solutions to men in different conditions. When homosexuals come to Christ, it has to be said that homosexual temptation after conversion is still likely. So homosexuals in their various conditions are called by Christ to learn sexual purity, given their particular circumstances.

First, in working with homosexuals, it quickly becomes evident that some of them have been effeminate, or attracted to men in some way, from a very early age. As long as they can remember, they have been "different." Whether this is the result of their physical constitution, or upbringing, or both, is immaterial. The fact remains that, as they say, they cannot imagine being attracted to a woman sexually. There are two issues here. One is the lack of interest in women, and the other is the prohibited interest in men. With regard to the first, scripturally speaking, the Bible does not require that a man have a sexual interest in women. This is the norm, but no law is being broken when that interest is not there.

So under these circumstances, the sexual interest in men must be resisted like any other temptation. God requires sexual purity, both in thought and deed, and such a man is like a man with heterosexual temptations with no immediate possibility of marriage. Lust is always prohibited. If it is true that such a man could not be interested sexually in a woman, then he needs to come to understand that God's will for him is celibacy. The only lawful sexual partner for him would be a woman, and if that is not possible, then he is called to have no sexual partner. This is difficult for many moderns to accept because we have come to believe that access to orgasms is somehow a divinely bestowed right. If it is true that he is "made" so that he cannot be married to a woman, then it is also true that he is called by the law of God to celibacy. This is a hard road, but it at least has the advantage of being clear and easy to understand.

But there is another kind of homosexual. This is the man who has been homosexual in practice, and has learned all kinds of bad sexual habits, but his homosexuality does not go to the bone. This condition may come about in many different ways. He may have been muddled up in a sex ed class during adolesence (a confusing time for most boys sexually anyway), he may have been seduced by someone, he may have wandered into the practice out of sheer sexual curiosity, and so forth.

But the central problem here is one of sexual laziness. A woman does not respond sexually in the same way a man does. Another man, on the other hand, responds in exactly the same way. A man and a woman are completely different sexually, but complementary. Learning *how* they may complement each other takes a great deal of love, time, childrearing, money, commitment, work, discipline, not to mention lots of practice under the covers. In bed, a man and a woman are two different musical notes, and it is their task to make harmony together. The man is to be utterly unlike the woman; the woman is to be utterly unlike the man. Nevertheless, the goal is to have the notes *blend*.

But singing harmony is harder than singing unison. A lazy man wants a partner who is just like he is. When it comes to sexual encounters, this is only possible with women who are willing to pretend they are not women for a fee—the women in porn or whores. But there is another kind of sexual partner who does not have to pretend; he *is* just the same way because he is another man. One man wants instant gratification; so does the other one. One man wants it now; so does the other one. Men in this condition are much more likely to call themselves bisexual; they are not looking for a true sexual partner, but just someone who is willing to help them get a quick release. It doesn't matter to them whether that person is a man or a woman.

When a man has wandered into homosexual practices

because of such factors, his problem is a lack of self-control, and what he really needs to learn is biblical sexual discipline. Given that the problem is a lack of biblical direction and discipline for his sexual interests, he is much more likely to learn *that* discipline sooner than the first kind of homosexual we discussed. As the grace of God takes root in his life, faithful marriage to one woman becomes a real option.

Now we have seen that the Bible teaches that homosexuality is a sin, and that those who live in such sin are excluded from the kingdom of God. But many are tempted to set aside the teaching of the Bible on this point because they have also heard that the Bible requires the death penalty for homosexuality, and surely *that* can't be acceptable to us here in the modern world.

In the Old Testament, we do see how God requires the suppression of various forms of sodomy in the civil realm. The problem was caused by the rampant homosexuality of the Canaanites, those who had inhabited the land before the Israelites—

> For they also built them high places, and images, and groves, on every high hill, and under every green tree. And there were also sodomites in the land: and they did according to all the abominations of the nations which the Lord cast out before the children of Israel. (1 Kgs. 14:23–24).

The sodomites in the land were carrying on a long sexual tradition practiced by the Canaanites before them.

God not only prohibits the activity, but He also assigns a penalty to it: "Thou shalt not lie with mankind, as with womankind: it is abomination" (Lev. 18:22). This is followed a few chapters later with the requirement that such be executed: "If a man also lie with mankind, as he lieth with a woman, both of them have committed an abomination: they shall surely be put to death; their blood shall be upon them" (Lev. 20:13). At the very least, this should show us how serious a sin this is.

At the same time, some have taken this as a *mandatory* biblical requirement that all forms of homosexuality receive the death penalty. But if we take all of Scripture into account, this cannot be the meaning of the law. Centuries later, we find this: "And Asa did that which was right in the eyes of the Lord, as did David his father. And he took away the sodomites out of the land, and removed all the idols that his fathers had made" (1 Kgs. 15:11–12). Asa is described here *as doing what is right*, and yet what he does is banish sodomites, not execute them. A short time later, Jehoshaphat does the same thing: "And the remnant of the sodomites, which remained in the days of his father Asa, he took out of the land" (1 Kgs. 22:46). Jehoshaphat was a godly king, and his treatment of the sodomites was exile, not the death penalty.

But how is this to be reconciled with the law from Leviticus 20? Two possibilities should be considered. The first is that the law is setting the maximum penalty allowed, not the minimum penalty. In other words, the Bible requires the suppression of homosexual vice, with the tools for such restriction including the possibility of the death penalty, but also allowing for banishment. Death is not necessarily an unjust punishment, but lawful punishments shy of that are certainly endorsed by Scripture as well. This is, I think, the preferred option.

But the second possibility is that a certain form of homosexual behavior is being addressed by the Levitical law, that is, anal intercourse. When a man lies with a man *as with a woman*, then he and his partner will surely be put to death. Other forms of sexual perversions between males would not incur the death penalty. Of the two options I think this is by far the less likely.

Modern Christians are finding themselves increasingly surrounded by a sodomite culture. This has happened, in part, because we have not studied what the Bible teaches, or, having studied it, are not willing to accept it. Whether we are considering the problem of sodomy on a personal level, or on a civil level, we will not come to sexual wisdom until we come to realize that God hates all homosexual practice, and that the fear of the Lord is to hate what He hates. Compassion for the sodomite, and a willingness to present the gospel to him, is not inconsistent with a true hatred for the perversion. The examples of Scripture are not given to us for nothing—"Even as Sodom and Gomorrha, and the cities about them in like manner, giving themselves over to fornication, and going after strange flesh, are set forth for an example, suffering the vengeance of eternal fire" (Jude 7; cf. 2 Pet. 2:6).

Untamed, the flames of sexual desire lead to another kind of fire entirely.

CHAPTER TEN

Masturbation

We are to answer the questions surrounding masturbation the same way we seek to answer *all* questions—"What does the Bible say?" Interestingly, the Bible says nothing at all about it directly, and because of this our chapter must be comparatively short. This biblical silence cannot be explained by attributing a prudish silence to the biblical writers. They were not shy about condemning all kinds of sexual practices—sex with your grandchildren (Lev. 18:10), sex with your stepmother (1 Cor. 5:1), sex with your barnyard animals (Lev. 18:23), and so forth. No, the silence of the Bible on this subject is not an *embarrassed* silence. If God had wanted to prohibit the practice outright, it would have been easy enough to do. The silence of the Bible on this is singular.

So following Scripture, we cannot say directly that masturbation in itself is a sin. In order to prohibit the practice outright, we would need some sort of scriptural case for prohibiting it outright. The Bible either would have to prohibit it directly, or we would have to be able to show its sinfulness by reasoning from biblical premises by good and necessary consequence. The former is not the case, but, with regard to the latter, we can say that we are almost there and at least have enough biblical direction to discourage the practice.

This is because we *are* able to say quite a bit about

those things which usually lead to masturbation and which generally make it necessary. Consequently, biblical wisdom requires that masturbation be discouraged, even though we cannot say that a man is *necessarily* sinning if he does. If a man is careful to avoid the lust prohibited by Christ and His apostles, most (if not all) of the occasions where masturbation seems like a *need* will have been removed. The principle here is that "all things are lawful unto me, but all things are not expedient: all things are lawful for me, but I will not be brought under the power of any" (1 Cor. 6:12). That masturbation has the capacity to enslave is not disputed by anyone, and so even if a man has decided that it is lawful in some cases, a refusal to be brought under its authority is still to be encouraged. And this relates to another point that should be made here about that which is "lawful but not necessary." Just because something is lawful does not mean that the wise should make a point of doing it. Hitting yourself on the head with a hammer is lawful.

Teachers I respect do differ on this issue of masturbation. Some maintain that in rare cases a man can relieve himself without unlawful lust. Others maintain that sinful lust is the *sine qua non* of masturbation. But even assuming for the sake of our discussion that a man is capable of relieving himself physically without using an unlawful lust as fuel, at the same time, if he is wise, he will be very sparing in resorting to masturbation. I would want to encourage him to learn to abstain from it altogether. We have already mentioned the *grace* of learning self-discipline in this area.

One reason for discouraging it is that a single man who has masturbated habitually for years before getting married is really not preparing himself for a sexual relationship with a *woman*. Masturbation is lousy preparation for genuine lovemaking. Further, it is good preparation for sexual incompetence in learning to satisfy a woman.

In this respect, masturbation could even be considered

an odd form of "homosexuality." If every sexual experience a man has had for the last ten years has been without a woman, then his only experience of sex is with a male (himself). But when he gets married, his wife will not be nearly as responsive to his every whim as *he* used to be. "So what's wrong with *her*?" he might come to wonder. Put another way, habitual or frequent masturbation is a very poor preparation for marriage. Fortunately, if a man avoids what *is* directly condemned as sin by the Bible (i.e., the lust), then he should not have this problem. If he still masturbates occasionally, then he should not stress over it—but he should at the same time strive to avoid it in the future and keep his eye on the pattern of his life. In this area, self-deception is terribly easy, and genuine accountability terribly difficult.

A young man who takes this advice and sets a course of sexual self-discipline for himself should keep certain principles in mind. First, physical helps are helps, not final solutions. Self-control is part of the fruit of the Spirit, and our sexual sanctification does not operate differently than the other aspects of our sanctification. Sexual self-control is a work of the *grace* of God (Eph. 2:10). Secondly, what the Bible teaches about sex and lust should be studied and memorized. When temptation hits, Scripture that applies to the situation should be immediately available. This is how Jesus resisted temptation, and we should follow His example. Many passages cited throughout this book should be committed to memory for the purpose of applying them while standing in the checkout line at the supermarket: "I am quite convinced that her breasts are none of my business. Hebrews 13:4." Third, a man should not ever look at images which could serve as lustful fuel *at any time.* In other words, just because masturbation does not occur immediately does not mean that the images are not a major factor later on. For example, a man might watch a movie with way too much skin in it and yet not masturbate that night. He thinks he is okay. But these images are nevertheless now part of his storehouse of lust, and he can conveniently forget how they got there. In the grip of self-deception, a man might spend a lot of time stocking his storehouse and yet believe that what he is doing "does not affect him." In this he is grossly self-deceived and well on his way to becoming a mouth-breather. Lastly, he should know when he is most vulnerable and take steps to limit his time in those situations. If he has trouble in the shower, he should take short showers. If he has trouble when he wakes up in the morning, he should establish some early morning commitments, and so forth.

The same goes for married men who are temporarily "single." The same basic principles apply to them, although with a few differences. If a man is away from his wife for an extended period, he should take special care that he stay away from lust and all the occasions of it. Although he might think that masturbation could provide help in keeping such sexual distractions at bay, it is far more likely that masturbation will serve as gasoline on the sexual fire and not as the hoped for water. Further, a married man can develop the same kinds of bad sexual habits that a single man can. This is particularly the case if the husband is in any way dissatisfied with his sexual relationship. He can find himself turning to himself even when there is no external reason. He is not on a business trip, but his wife was unreponsive to his advances. Instead of doing what he ought to do, if he is sexually lazy, he will head off to the bathroom to take care of himself.

But during times of enforced separation, there are some differences for married men. First, he is accustomed to an ongoing sexual relationship and so the necessity of physical relief may sometimes seem to be much more of a pressing need for him. He may have a case of blue balls and be more interested in walking than in women. Also, unlike a single man, he has a number of lawful "memories" available to him. Even so, the same principles mentioned earlier still apply. It should always be remembered that in this entire area, the ease with which we fall into self-deception is remarkable. For example, a selfish man could glibly tell himself that he is only taking care of himself so that he will be a better husband while on the road. Way to sacrifice, big guy. A married man should recognize that he has a serious problem with this if he finds a temptation to masturbate when he is not away from home. And all men, single or married, should recognize that solitary sex is *not* the normative biblical pattern. Recalling that the love between a man and a woman is a picture of Christ and the church, we should note that, quite apart from the moral and self-discipline issues involved, masturbation is lousy theology.

In conclusion, it is worth noting that in Old Testament Israel, sexual activity made a man ritually unclean. To a very limited extent, the fact of sexual relations resulted in a public condition:

> And if any man's seed of copulation go out from him, then he shall wash all his flesh in water, and be unclean until the even. And every garment, and every skin, whereon is the seed of copulation, shall be washed with water, and be unclean until the even. The woman also with whom man shall lie with seed of copulation, they shall both bathe themselves in water, and be unclean until the even. (Lev. 15:16–18)

Under the new covenant, we do not have this restriction—for which we are all glad. But it is worth noting that a young Israelite who had a problem with masturbation would not really have the option of keeping the fact secret. If there was an emission of semen, he was ritually unclean and this had public ramifications. And if he had no wife, there was likely to be a good deal of yukking it up at his expense in the surrounding tents.

CHAPTER ELEVEN

Celibacy

While it may seem unlikely to us now, we should prepare for a resurgence in the popularity of celibacy, and for the same reasons it became widespread in the early centuries of the Church. Any culture which gets itself into a sexually pathological condition is simply inviting over-reaction. That was the decadent state of affairs in the late Roman Empire, and that is our condition now. But after a people have seen everything and done most of it, sometimes twice, we should not be surprised when a massive sexual *ennui* sets in. Seen in this light, celibacy is a form of sexuality, not a denial of it, and so it warrants some consideration in a book like this.

This form of celibacy is a reaction and is not the celibacy commended by biblical writers. So one of the first things we must do is distinguish the two. This is because our current modernist wisdom requires us to hold that the right to an orgasm is a basic civil right, and this in turn requires us hold that all forms of celibacy be lumped together in one big pathetic category.

But this does an injustice to the biblical data. The first thing we must acknowledge is that celibacy (of a certain kind) is commended in the Bible. We have to take care that we do not combine our historical Protestant antipathy for the excesses of ascetic monks with our modernist compromises with every current sexual gospel, and then as a result conclude that the Bible could not possibly commend a life of celibacy. Most modern evangelicals know that the apostle Paul was gifted with celibacy, but this is seen as a personal thing (kind of a "Paul" thing) and certainly not intended as a subcultural movement within the faith. This is why we rush to categorize people as "singles," and we quietly assume them to be sexually marooned, not sexually dedicated.

Now there is an asceticism which is useless in restraining the desires of the flesh. Paul tells us:

> Wherefore if ye be dead with Christ from the rudiments of the world, why, as though living in the world, are ye subject to ordinances, (Touch not; taste not; handle not; which all are to perish with the using;) after the commandments and doctrines of men? Which things have indeed a shew of wisdom in will worship, and humility, and neglecting of the body; not in any honour to the satisfying of the flesh. (Col. 2:20–23)

There is a way of neglecting the body, in other words, and treating it harshly, which does not check the flesh— rather, it *is* the flesh. Men take a certain perverse pride in mortifying themselves in this way. From this warning, we quickly reject any form of bodily discipline that is spiritual in nature. But the fact that asceticism can go off the rails does not mean that every form of ascetic discipline is worthless. Our Lord fasted for forty days and nights. And His predecessor lived in a somewhat austere fashion, not eating or drinking the way the Lord did—"And John was clothed with camel's hair, and with a girdle of a skin about his loins; and he did eat locusts and wild honey" (Mk. 1:6). This was not a middle class suburban existence. John the Baptist was not married; he lived in the desert as an Old Covenant monk.

We see something similar with a woman who was one of the first to greet the Lord on his arrival in the world:

> And there was one Anna, a prophetess, the daughter of
> Phanuel, of the tribe of Aser: she was of a great age, and
> had lived with an husband seven years from her virginity;
> and she was a widow of about fourscore and four years,
> which departed not from the temple, but served God with
> fastings and prayers night and day. (Lk. 2:36)

This woman had been married for seven years, but after
the death of her husband she dedicated herself to the worship of God in His temple. In no way was this decision of
hers criticized or mocked in the biblical account.

Some might object that these are simply historical examples, and that we should not try to build doctrine out of
narrative. All right, then:

> His disciples say unto him, If the case of the man be so
> with his wife, it is not good to marry. But he said unto
> them, All men cannot receive this saying, save they to
> whom it is given. For there are some eunuchs, which were
> so born from their mother's womb: and there are some
> eunuchs, which were made eunuchs of men: and there be
> eunuchs, which have made themselves eunuchs for the
> kingdom of heaven's sake. He that is able to receive it, let
> him receive it. (Mt. 19:10–12)

Jesus had just finished giving them some hard words
on the nature of Christian discipleship within marriage.
The disciples reacted with astonishment—if *that* is the way
Christian marriage is, then perhaps it would be better to
be unmarried. Jesus agrees—perhaps. Some eunuchs are
that way from birth. Some are made eunuchs by men for
various reasons. For example, the great medieval thinker
Abelard was castrated because of his fornication with
Heloise. Many others, the *castrati*, were made that way so
that they could be devoted to their music, and keep their
voices from changing. But Jesus goes on to a third category—those who forswear sexual relations for the sake
of the kingdom of heaven. The way of the kingdom in marriage is hard. So is the other way. Those who are able to
hear it should hear it.

It is plain that celibacy in the kingdom is not the "once in a blue moon" thing it is sometimes represented as being. Those who are called, who can handle it, should do so. Those who cannot, should not. But the way of discipleship for them is simply different, not easy. To the married, Paul says:

> Defraud ye not one the other, except it be with consent for a time, that ye may give yourselves to fasting and prayer; and come together again, that Satan tempt you not for your incontinency. But I speak this by permission, and not of commandment. For I would that all men were even as I myself. But every man hath his proper gift of God, one after this manner, and another after that. (1 Cor. 7:5–7)

Paul gives permission to married couples to pull away from sexual relations for a time. We see this kind of temporary celibacy in the Old Testament as well. Before God revealed Himself to the people at Mt. Sinai, He told them to "come not at your wives" (Exod. 19:15). But Paul tells the Corinthians to keep their sexual "fasts" short, otherwise they will be tempted to some kind of fornication. He emphasizes that he is giving permission for these fasts; he is not requiring them. He knows that all men are not like he is, which is fine with him. At the same time, he has been so blessed in his gift that he wishes that all men could experience it. Nevertheless, he knows that in the providence of God it is not right to question God's judgments. It is not as though he is gifted and the men who must have sex are not gifted. Rather, the difference is a difference in gifts. One man must please a woman in bed, and another man must not. One man is to be given to the pleasures and duties of loving a wife, and another man is set free from the cares and distraction of caring for a wife. It would be good if those moderns who are "sexually active" (what an awful phrase!) would show the same wisdom that Paul shows here. He enjoys his gift, but is not imperialistic with it. Those of us who are married should enjoy our gift as well, but recognize that in the Bible there are people who are sexually dedicated to God and that this is not an aberration. Again, this is different than the unbeliever who adopts "celibacy" because he is sexually weary. It is also different from the individual who is celibate from necessity—unmarried, not because of dedication to Christ, but unmarried because a lack of self-control in his life has managed to create a loser that no self-respecting woman would want to marry.

This brings us to another category of celibates in the Bible, the office of widow. In our parlance, a widow is a woman who has lost her husband. In the language of the early church, this usage was current also, but there was an additional way for the word *widow* to be used. A widow in this second sense was a woman who was enrolled as a widow and was cared for by the church. In other words, *widow* was a type of office—similar to that held by Anna, mentioned earlier—

> Honour widows that are widows indeed. But if any widow have children or nephews, let them learn first to shew piety at home, and to requite their parents: for that is good and acceptable before God. Now she that is a widow indeed, and desolate, trusteth in God, and continueth in supplications and prayers night and day. But she that liveth in pleasure is dead while she liveth. And these things give in charge, that they may be blameless. But if any provide not for his own, and specially for those of his own house, he hath denied the faith, and is worse than an infidel. Let not a widow be taken into the number under threescore years old, having been the wife of one man, well reported of for good works; if she have brought up children, if she have lodged strangers, if she have washed the saints' feet, if she have relieved the afflicted, if she have diligently followed every good work. But the younger widows refuse: for when they have begun to wax wanton against Christ, they will marry; having damnation, because they have cast off their first faith. And withal they learn to be idle, wandering about from house to house; and not only idle, but tattlers

also and busybodies, speaking things which they ought not. I will therefore that the younger women marry, bear children, guide the house, give none occasion to the adversary to speak reproachfully. For some are already turned aside after Satan. If any man or woman that believeth have widows, let them relieve them, and let not the church be charged; that it may relieve them that are widows indeed. (1 Tim. 5:3–16)

I do not wish to be misunderstood here, but what we are talking about is a kind of *nun*. The use of this word in this setting is unsettling to Roman Catholics because of the requirements that Paul places upon any such sexual dedication to Christ. The word is unsettling to Protestants because it is used at all. But consider what Paul is actually requiring here.

First, he is in no rush to recruit women to this office. If there is a way for her family to care for her, then that is the way it should go. He comments in passing that a "widow indeed" is very much like Anna, devoted to God, devoted to prayer and supplication, night and day. A widow who gives herself to pleasure is dead while she lives. Paul then returns to emphasize that the household should take care of this woman, and not to do so is a practical denial of the faith.

Paul then proceeds to talk about the qualifications that any woman must meet before she can be enrolled as a widow. But before addressing this, we must see that we are in fact talking about sexual dedication to Christ. Paul says here, in urging the rejection of younger widows from enrollment, that they will at some point want to marry and he interprets this as waxing "wanton against Christ." In other words, it is clear that to be enrolled as a widow, there had to be a vow of celibacy which a young widow would be much more likely to break. Further, this vow of celibacy, if broken, would bring down damnation on the woman's head, and was interpreted as equivalent to casting off the faith. This is not a problem brought about through a second marriage, because a second marriage is precisely what Paul urges as the solution for such younger widows. They should marry, he says, and take care of their homes. It is the result of a second marriage after enrollment as a widow. If enrollment as a widow were nothing more than a financial support of needy women in the congregation, then there would be no problem with a woman losing her husband after ten years, being cared for by the church for three years, and then marrying again. But Paul saw this as apostasy, and there is no way to comprehend his response without seeing that the woman was bound to Christ in some peculiar way, having taken a vow of celibacy, having taken a vow not to marry. If she had not done so, there could be no problem with her marrying. But there was a problem with her remarrying, and therefore she must have been bound in some way not to do so.

But the problem is even greater for the Roman Catholic understanding of the role of a nun. What does Paul require here before a woman may be permitted to take this vow? The widow must be at least sixty years old. She had to have been the wife of one man, vigorous in good works, a godly mother, and hospitable. In other words, to put it bluntly, a woman could not be a nun unless she had forty years experience in lovemaking, cooking, wiping noses, entertaining strangers, and all the rest of it.

Another form of celibacy *may* be found in Scriptures, but here, the point is not so clear. Perhaps the best way to introduce the subject is through quoting a translation offered by the New English Bible of 1 Corinthians 7:36–38:

> In saying this I have no wish to keep you on a tight rein. I am thinking simply of your own good, of what is seemly, and of your freedom to wait upon the Lord without distraction. But if a man has *a partner in celibacy* and feels that he is not behaving properly towards her, if, that is, his instincts are too strong for him, and something must be done, he may do as he pleases; there is nothing wrong in it; let them marry. But if a man is steadfast in his purpose,

being under no compulsion, and has complete control of his own choice; and if he has decided to his own mind to preserve his partner in her virginity, he will do well. Thus, he who marries his partner does well, and he who does not will do better.

In the early Church a practice surrounding celibacy arose at some point, and the translators of the New English Bible thought Paul's comments in this passage were a reference to it. Men and women began living together in celibate "marriage," with the women involved called *subintroductae*. Their Greek name was *suneiskatoi*, and this practice was a considerable nuisance to the early bishop at Constantiople, John Chrysostom.

Speaking of the great experiment of "sublimation," as he calls it, Charles Williams simply assumes this understanding of the passage, and says,

> "In some cases it failed. But we know nothing—most unfortunately—of the cases in which it did not fail, and that there were such cases seems clear from St. Paul's quite simple acceptance of the idea. By the time of Cyprian, Bishop of Carthage in the third century, the ecclesiastical authories were much more doubtful. The women—subintroductae as they were called—apparently slept with their companions without intercourse; Cyprian does not exactly disbelieve them, but he discourages the practice. And the Synod of Elvira (305) and the Council of Nicaea (325) forbade it altogether. The great experiment had to be abandoned because of 'scandal'." (Williams, *Descent of the Dove* [Grand Rapids, MI: Eerdmans, 1939], pp. 12–13)

Williams is quite right about the attitude of the Church fathers toward this practice and about the fact that it was a practice. Of course, this oddity in the early Church could be filed along with many other temporary oddities were it not for the possibility that the practice began in the apostolic era, and gained the support (however grudging) of the apostle Paul. So it matters what this passage actually says and how it is to be interpreted. But whether Paul was speaking of it is open to question—

> But if any man think that he behaveth himself uncomely toward his virgin, if she pass the flower of her age, and need so require, let him do what he will, he sinneth not: let them marry. Nevertheless he that standeth stedfast in his heart, having no necessity, but hath power over his own will, and hath so decreed in his heart that he will keep his virgin, doeth well. So then he that giveth her in marriage doeth well; but he that giveth her not in marriage doeth better. (1 Cor. 7:36–38)

The most common interpretation of this is that it is speaking of a father and his daughter, and concerns whether he should give her in marriage or not. This is borne out by the verb that is used in v. 38, which means *to give in marriage* (cf. Mt. 22:30; 24:38; Lk. 17:27). The problem with this is the language used earlier, which seems somewhat unusual if talking about a father and daughter (behaving uncomely, power over his own will, and so forth). The other possible problem concerns the actual advice given. If this is a father/daughter relationship, then Paul appears to be strongly urging the fathers to not give their daughters away in marriage. If interpreted this way, we should be careful to note the advice was governed by the peculiar circumstances of the era, as Paul put it earlier, because of the present distress (v. 26). Taken this way, Paul is not teaching about the permanent sexual state of affairs for the Church. He is simply saying that if a man can avoid being married during a time of fiery persecution, that would be a wise thing to do. But it would be better, he says, to be married during persecution than to be sexually immoral during such a time. Marriage is not a sin even when it might be prudent to avoid it.

So all things considered, it is not clear that Paul is talking about celibate partnerships. Such things are certainly consistent with the climate of the culture and church several centuries later, but to have such a daring sexual experiment going on under apostolic oversight stretches credulity. But if Paul *is* talking about the practice of celibate partnerships, it is noteworthy that he is very concerned about the possibility of scandal, and teaches that to end the celibate experiment in marriage is not a sin. So while the apostolic Church included celibacy in very limited contexts, it would be wrong to see celibacy as the norm during the first century. It was not unheard of, and there was a place for it in the Church, but neither was it the pattern for the average member of the Church. Even when persecution made it somewhat of a quasi-norm, Paul maintains the clear biblical understanding that it is not good for man to be alone.

With this consideration of biblical celibacy behind us, we need to briefly conclude by addressing unbiblical forms of it. Although I am painting with a broad brush here, I want to consider two ungodly reasons why a man might remain single—though it hardly seems fair to dignify these reasons with the honorable word *celibacy*. In our culture, among those who remain unattached to a woman, I believe these two reasons are not at all uncommon. Remember, we are not considering celibacy itself, but rather celibacy for ungodly reasons. Celibacy considered in itself can be a godly calling: "But I would have you without carefulness. He that is unmarried careth for the things that belong to the Lord, how he may please the Lord" (1 Cor. 7:32).

The first cause of this kind of ungodly celibacy is *laziness*. If a man is unmarried so that he may devote himself to kingdom work, that is one thing. But if he has an easy job, a nice apartment, free weekends, no hassles, and so forth, this is a state of affairs that some men could grow to like very much. Of course many men struggle with loneliness and sexual temptation, but others really come to like the lack of entanglements. But the reason they like it this way is that it provides lots of time to watch football games and movie videos. God has called us to work diligently before Him in all that we do, and many men learn how to do this through the responsibilities that marriage and fatherhood bring. Another honorable route is for a single man to give himself wholeheartedly to the work God has assigned to him. But to drift into a lifestyle which places maximum value on recreation and entertainment, with work seen as only that necessary evil which makes it possible to earn enough money to buy concert tickets, is a tragic waste of a human life. Laziness is a very common temptation to the male sex, but it is one which threatens true masculinity. More men are likely to "unman" themselves through laziness than through many other sins.

The second cause of undesirable celibacy would best be described as *resentment* and *wounded pride*. Men do not take rejection very well, and if a man has been in an unfortunate relationship, or was dumped by a woman, or a woman was unfaithful to him, he may find it very easy to withdraw from any kind of significant interaction between the sexes. His resentment cycles downward, and after a time, he may find himself in a position of being unable to approach a woman.

Some men in this position really are celibate; that is, they do not have any relationship with any women. They withdraw because they are wounded. Other men with a similar attitude may be sexually promiscuous (and therefore not celibate), but they *are* emotionally celibate. They are hostile to women and simply use them. Because their sexual vanity was hurt by a woman, they assume they have a license to destroy and hurt other women. For those who are so inclined, sex is an effective weapon. But ultimately it destroys everyone involved.

Those men who are single through no sin of theirs, but also through no *choice* of theirs, must learn to follow Christ in the midst of a difficult situation. They are not gifted with the permanent gift of celibacy, but they have been given that gift temporarily. God does not place His children in situations where faithfulness to Him is impossible. This means that if a man is twenty years old, and will not be married for four more years, the grace is available to him to live faithfully as a temporary celibate. The fact that he must turn to God constantly for that grace shows him that he has not been gifted as Paul was, with a settled mind on the matter, but the grace of God is available to him.

So then, the Bible teaches that some men may be called to celibacy, eunuchs for the sake of the kingdom, but they should make sure they are fully settled in their own minds. Others, in the providence of God, are temporarily celibate, and even though they do not have the "permanent" gift, grace is available to them to live *pure* celibate lives until the time God calls them to marriage. For the rest, they should get serious about finding a godly Christian wife to sleep with.

CHAPTER TWELVE

Sexual Solutions

In no way does the biblical marriage bed exclude a highly-charged eroticism. But beyond the honeymoon period, biblical eroticism requires discipline and hard work. An undisciplined man does not want to be troubled by such labors; he wants simply to follow his testosterone wherever it leads. If thrilling sex is there, he takes it. If it is not, he wonders "how come?" Good sex is assumed to be something guaranteed to him by the Bill of Rights.

The need for sexual discipline can be seen in many interesting ways. One interesting passage in Corinthians teaches us much more than the simple fact that husband and wife ought to have sexual relations. The really intriguing word in this passage is *authority*—

> Now concerning the things whereof ye wrote unto me: It is good for a man not to touch a woman. Nevertheless, *to avoid fornication*, let every man have his own wife, and let every woman have her own husband. Let the husband render unto the wife due benevolence: and likewise also the wife unto the husband. *The wife hath not power* of her own body, but the husband: and likewise also *the husband hath not power* of his own body, but the wife. Defraud ye not one the other, except it be with consent for a time, that ye may give yourselves to fasting and prayer; and come together again, that Satan tempt you not for your incontinency. (1 Cor. 7:1–5)

Paul is saying that a husband and wife ought to have regular sexual relations in order to protect themselves against immorality. But much more than regularity is involved. Why is it that many men who have ongoing relations with their wives do *not* experience any of the protection God intends for them to have? The answer is found in that word *authority*. He has authority over her body, and interestingly, Paul teaches that she has authority over his. As the head of the house, he is responsible for everything that happens in the home, and for the state of everything, including the state of their sex life. He is responsible for his authority over her, but he is also responsible for hers over him.

Now, what is he to teach her? In the discussion which follows, I am not saying that everything described is somehow biblically *required*. If neither husband or wife are interested in what the Bible allows here, then we may presume they are both sexually content, and the husband is probably not reading this book. That is fine. But if he is thinking about "how it would be wonderful if she would only . . ." but then shakes his head because she would never go for *that*, then he needs to learn that these things are his responsibility. It is his responsibility to go one of two directions—either to learn that his desire is wrongheaded and needs to be dropped or to teach his wife how she may meet it.

His faithfulness to her provides the security she needs in order to be taught by him. He bound himself to that faithfulness with a vow when they got married. He needs also, as necessary, to make a covenant with his eyes, so that he will not wander: "I have made a covenant with mine eyes; why then should I think upon a maid?" (Job 31:1). His faithfulness to one woman is a necessary foundation for him to be able to teach that one woman.

Earlier I mentioned that Christians should not be importing weirdness to the marriage bed for the sake of some high octane kick. That is all very well, but who defines weirdness? *By what standard?* As Christians we are to define what we do and what we avoid doing according to the pattern found in Scripture. What are the limits of propriety within the marriage bed according to Scripture? As we discuss the examples of godly eroticism provided in Scripture, we should find more than enough material to offend both the prudish and the decadent.

In the Song of Solomon we find much more than just the sense of touch. Both taste and smell are involved in lovemaking: "Let him kiss me with the kisses of his mouth: for thy love is better than wine" (1:2). Fragrant ointments are used to enhance the experience (1:13). The appearance of the bed and of the room matter a great deal: "Also our bed is green. The beams of our house are cedar, and our rafters of fir" (1:16b–17). Passionate kissing—French kissing—is clearly described. Honey and milk are under her tongue; he knows this because he has tasted her there (4:11). The poetry is pastoral, frequently set in idyllic meadows or gardens. The couple are able to fantasize about being elsewhere, making love outdoors, for example (7:11–12). The lovers are very much interested in one another's bodies—everywhere. For example, he is drawn to her feet, her thighs, her navel, her waist, her breasts, her mouth (4:5; 7:1–3). She is described as a garden (4:12), and her sexual organs are described as an enclosed garden within a garden. She wants the wind to blow on her garden so that her lover will come into it and *taste* it (4:16). Conversely, she delights to taste his fruit as well (2:3). Obviously, this oral foreplay is not limited to kissing one another on pursed lips, and both the man and the woman enjoy tasting one another.

Passionate, intense lovemaking seems clearly lawful, up to and including oral foreplay. But even here a biblical couple have to guard themselves against the world's demands for an *autonomous* sexual pleasure world. An oral sexual *union* is no substitute for God's design—worldlings pursue this kind of thing in hope of some extra thrill. And neither should a couple fall into such practices in a way that degrades or humiliates. In the Song of Solomon, the descriptions of such activities are clearly in the context of intense foreplay leading to a normal coital union. There are limits to their fantasizing as well. Fantasy is clearly part of any poetic lovemaking, and so it is lawful to fantasize. But it is not lawful to fantasize about being with someone else, or with your spouse so altered by the "plastic surgery of the mind" as to be someone else. Nor should a husband and wife fantasize about each other in a way that runs contrary to God's law—for example, imagining themselves having sexual relations before or outside of marriage. If God doesn't want us to do it, He doesn't want us to get pleasure from *thinking* about doing it. And if the imagination is of some lawful activity, it would be far better for the couple to discipline themselves by using the fantasy to learn to do what they like to imagine doing. At the same time, fantasizing about something like a change of location is something which can be clearly seen in the Song of Solomon.

The lovemaking of this biblical couple is clearly not occuring in the dark under six or seven blankets. This couple is very open with one another and take a great sexual delight in their communion. This delight concentrates on specifics and is not just a general approval of sex, whatever that is. The descriptions given are poetic, not pornographic, and yet at the same time, the descriptions are unambiguous, particularly in the original. Sometimes our translators have taken the more tasteful, albeit less accurate, route.

More than one passage points toward a double meaning. For example, consider the place where the beloved sought entry to her room, but she was initially unwilling: "My beloved put in his hand by the hole of the door, and my bowels were moved for him. I rose up to open to my beloved . . ." (Song 5:4–5). But this could also be rendered, "My beloved thrust his 'hand' through the hole; my vagina was inflamed, I arose and opened. . . ." In 7:2, the woman's navel is possibly her vulva. And when the woman is speaking of her lover, she delights in him in a similar way: "His hands are as gold rings set with the beryl: his belly is as bright ivory overlaid with sapphires" (Song 5:14). His "belly" here probably refers to his phallus, considered by her as a tusk of ivory. In short, this couple are really into it—the literal meaning at 5:1 is to be *drunk* with lovemaking. Within the confines of the marriage bed, a man and woman are called to drive one another out of their respective heads.

Such relationships do not "just happen." Discipline and work on all aspects of the relationship are absolutely necessary—focusing on sex alone (or first) will go nowhere. For those men who are interested in pursuing the broader issues involved in treating their wives right, they should obtain copies of the books *Reforming Marriage* and *Federal Husband* and then, after that, come back to this book. If they do not know how to live considerately with their wives throughout the course of their lives, then the information presented here will only be cause for further exasperation. But in the context of mutual affection and esteem, sex is supposed to be good.

When it is, this is a great protection for the man. Clearly a man who enjoys this kind of immense pleasure with his wife will have great difficulty turning elsewhere. A man sitting down to a steak dinner is unlikely to excuse himself in order to go eat some Ding Dongs he has stashed away in the closet. But a man facing yet another dinner of Twinkies might think about doing just that.

But before some husband says, "Yeah!" and runs off to show his wife this book with all her shortcomings highlighted, he must remember that *he* is responsible to teach and lead her gently. He cannot bully her or push her to do whatever it is that he wants. Remember the earlier example of the orangutuan playing the violin. But if he is not protected from sexual temptation by their sexual relationship, then neither can he just forget about it. He must love her and teach her. His teaching must encompass all of life—sexual instruction cannot come in isolation. He must learn from the Bible (*not* from his pornography, and *not* from unbelieving sex therapists), and then he must teach his wife from that same Bible. Now this is not to say that pornography gets everything wrong—real women really do have two breasts, just like in *Playboy*—or that the sexual therapists have everything wrong. It simply is to show that our supreme authority in everything we do must be Scripture. With that as a given, we are truly safeguarded, and we have a standard against which we may measure anything we may have learned elsewhere.

The overall atmosphere of the home is not just a protection for the wife, allowing her to grow and flourish sexually. It is also a protection for the husband. When he is leading her as he ought to be, she will respond to and respect him. *This respect is a tremendous sexual protection.* A man who is disrespected in his own home is vulnerable to another woman who will give him false respect—the flattering words of a seductress. But again, if he is not respected, then *he* is the one who must see that the situation is put right in his own home. If he does not do this, then he is vulnerable to the one who will give him false respect. In order to entice a man, a loose woman will use her fluttering eyes and her flattering tongue. She is not sincere with either, but hey, it works—

> For the commandment is a lamp; and the law is light; and reproofs of instruction are the way of life: To keep thee from the evil woman, *from the flattery of the tongue of a strange woman.* Lust not after her beauty in thine heart; neither let her take thee with her eyelids. For by means of a whorish woman a man is brought to a piece of bread: and the adulteress will hunt for the precious life. Can a man take fire in his bosom, and his clothes not be burned? Can one go upon hot coals, and his feet not be burned? So he that goeth in to his neighbour's wife; whosoever toucheth her shall not be innocent. (Prov. 6:23–29)

All these issues, and related issues, require a great deal of careful discussion between husband and wife. And that is not possible unless they are on good terms with one another, which really is the central protection within marriage.

Obviously some of the sexual questions which arise cannot be answered directly from Scripture. But where scriptural principles *can* be brought to bear, we must do so. Where nothing can be said scripturally about a practice, then we should seek to think in scriptural categories. Within these general guidelines, our assumption should be that "whatever it is" is lawful—but that does not make it necessary. If we learn our lessons, we might come to the point where we have as much fun as a biblical patriarch— "And it came to pass, when he had been there a long time, that Abimelech king of the Philistines looked out at a window, and saw, and, behold, Isaac was sporting with Rebekah his wife" (Gen. 26:8).

We are a fallen race, and so we understand bossiness fairly well. However, biblical headship is not well understood. A very common mistake is to confuse headship with bossiness. In our topic of discussion, men frequently confuse sexual headship with sexual bossiness. The former is required; the latter forbidden.

Many Christian husbands have erroneously assumed that because the Bible teaches the man is the head of the home, this must mean the wife has no covenantal authority over him. As we shall see, the assumption is false, but this does not keep it from being widespread. To take a common example in this area, suppose that a married man is defeated in some significant way by a problem with pornography. He knows that his behavior is sinful, and he confesses his sin (regularly) to God. In search of accountability, he may even have told a male Christian friend about it. But he also assumes that such information would only distress his wife and that he is not obligated to tell her anything about it because she is not the head of the home. This is

just an individual problem that "he has to work out."
But as we saw earlier, Scripture teaches us much more
than the simple fact that husband and wife ought to have
ongoing sexual relations. In this important respect, a Christian woman has authority over her husband—

> Nevertheless, to avoid fornication, let every man have his
> own wife, and let each woman have her own husband....
> The wife *hath not power* of her own body, but the husband:
> and likewise also the husband *hath not power* of his own
> body, but the wife. (1 Cor. 7:1–5)

Paul is certainly saying what most people glean from this
passage—a husband and wife ought to have regular sexual
relations in order to protect themselves against temptations
to immorality. But much more than regularity is involved.
Why is it that many men who have ongoing relations with
their wives do not experience the kind of protection God
intends for them to have? The answer is found in that word
authority. When the teaching of the passage is ignored, how
can we still expect the blessing promised in the passage?

The husband has authority over his wife's body, and
interestingly, Paul insists that she has a reciprocal authority over his. As the head of the house, he is responsible for
everything that happens in the home, including the state of
their sexual life together. He is responsible for his authority over her, and he is ultimately responsible for hers over
him. Nevertheless, she has genuine authority over him in
this area. The extent of their mutual authority is set by
Scripture and not by any rationalizing desires of the husband.

This means he must love her sexually as he wishes, and
he must teach her to wield a comparable biblical authority
over him sexually. If their relationship is to reflect the pattern found in Scripture, then he must teach her, and then
teach her to teach him. He must wield authority over her,
and expect her to wield authority over him. Many men are
vulnerable to the enticements of sexual sin simply because

their sexual lives are so boring that they think they need something extra to spice it up. Or, on their own authority, an authority they do not actually have, they are "rewarding" themselves because they feel shortchanged. Either way, turning away to sexual pleasure apart from home, even with the guilt, is easier for many men than taking responsibility for loving and teaching a wife.

Among other things, this means that a man is accountable to his wife for his sexual behavior. She has authority over him in this. Paul is saying far more than that the woman may initiate sexual relations with her husband. She certainly may do so, but she may do so for the reason which Paul gives. The reason given by the apostle is that a married woman has authority over the sexual behavior of her husband.

The ramifications of this are considerable. If a man has fallen in a sexual way, he does not have the authority on his own to decide whether his wife should be informed. His sexual behavior is her business, and she has authority over it. He has no authority to withhold from her what she would want to know.

Christian husbands often wonder why their wives have a problem with the Bible's teaching on submission. "What the Bible says on the subject is so plain! What is her problem?" But a man only has a good view of the authority he has over others when he has an equally good view of the authority he is under. This understanding provides a wonderful opportunity: A man can teach his wife submission through his own godly example of submission—why he can now show her how easy submission is!

If he refuses to submit to her where the Bible says she has authority, then he will have a hard time maintaining his dignity when he insists that she submit to his authority. A fundamental principle of biblical ethical behavior is that our actions are our declaration of what we expect others to do to us. This means many husbands must *want* unsubmissive wives.

Now getting the theology straight is one thing, and learning how that translates into every day problems in the marriage bed is another. How in *particular* must a man take leadership? We will begin this discussion by addressing those things which Christian husbands need to learn sexually, and then proceed to those things which their wives may need to be taught. This is the order we must take because unless the husband is studying and learning as he ought, there is little likelihood that his wife will be able to respond to him as well as he would like.

Before addressing this subject, I would refer the reader to consider again the earlier chapter on the biblical necessity of plain speaking. I want to say here what many Christian husbands need to hear, and it is my conviction that these things really cannot be communicated effectively any other way.

In order to make love to a woman, a man must be hard. This is obviously a physical truth, but an important metaphor is wrapped up in this as well. Any wimp can get an erection, but if he is an abdicating male, then his erection is really nothing but an irritating sexual hypocrisy. He is pretending to be, in a specific sexual situation, something which he is not throughout the rest of his life. In order to be sexually responsive, a wife needs to *respect*, on a fundamental level, the comprehensive masculinity of her husband. He must be a man, and not just a male. If he is aroused in the bedroom, that arousal must not make her resentment boil over—"Why can he not be aroused to do anything *else*?" This is not to say that this line of reasoning is something which a resentful wife would be able to articulate to herself. She may not be able to say exactly what the problem is. But this does not mean there is no connection. Simply put, if a man is not hard working, responsibile, diligent, courageous, and protective, then he should not act like he is in the bedroom. If his mind is soft, then he has no right to be hard.

In order to make love to a woman, a man must be

patient. But this is the patience of a craftsman waiting for his work to be done; it is not the patience of a fool waiting for lightning to strike. If a man and a woman live long enough together in the same house, and they do not positively hate each other, then there will periodically be good sex by accident. But in a good marriage, disciplined lovemaking is necessary to any consistent enjoyment of one another sexually. By disciplined lovemaking, I do not mean joyless sex, industriously pursued. The discipline required is that of the whole man and requires that he *not* approach the thing like an engineer. True, engineering is a discipline, but so is poetry. A man's patience should be evident in how he prepares for making love to his wife well before the start of the "official" proceedings. This includes how he speaks to her at breakfast the day before, how he speaks kindly of her to others in conversation, how he consistently acts as a conscientious head. Paul tells us that a man who loves his wife loves himself. Nowhere is this truth more obvious than in the sexual realm. A man who treats his wife with careful patience will enjoy enormous sexual dividends.

In order to make love to a woman, a man must be reasonable. When the Pharaoh wanted to show his contempt for the Israelites, he commanded them to make bricks without straw. In the same way, many men do not have any comprehension of the demands placed upon their wives during the course of the day. A Christian wife will be industrious, working hard through the day. She will be given to her nursing baby, overseeing her older children doing chores, getting the kids to and from school, and working around the home as she keeps everything together. This is what God requires of her (Tit. 2:4–5). Picture a long line of draining and exhausting demands, and there, standing last in line around 10:30 that night, is her fathead of a husband with bedroom eyes. *Then*, when the sex is not to his liking, he blames her. She is not responsive to his urgent needs apparently! The real problem is that he is not providing her with the resources she needs in order to be responsive. He must be reasonable, and if he wants certain things, he must plan for them with her in mind. He must be reasonable.

In order to make love to a woman, a man must be tender. Peter tells men to live considerately with their wives, as with a weaker vessel. This certainly has broader applications outside the bedroom, but it must be applied there as well. A simple-minded approach to the sexual difference between men and woman would say that he is tough and she is tender, he is hard and she is soft, and so forth. But this is just half the picture. As mentioned earlier, a man must be hard, but he must be soft at the same time. A woman is to be soft and responsive, but strength and passion are *not* out of place in her response. This means that a man must approach his wife with balance. In the context of his masculinity, he must be tender.

In order to make love to a woman, a man must be civilized. This is an area that requires careful thinking. I have mentioned several times earlier that a man should learn his sexual lessons from Scripture, and not from his pornographic primers. When men have had a problem with porn, or they have had a history with ungodly women, it is very easy for them to bring this experience into their marriage as kind of an unspoken standard. He remembers a prostitute who would do anything he wanted for an extra fifty bucks, and he does not understand why this "request" of his is so disdained by his wife. He has learned some pretty crude things from pornography and does not comprehend why his wife has a hang up over his suggestions that they try this or that.

Paul requires in Thessalonians that Christian men make love to their wives in a manner that is distinct from the "passionate lust" of the unbeliever. There is a similarity: sex is certainly sexual in both instances. But at the same time, Paul requires that a distinction between godly and ungodly sexuality be maintained in a Christian marriage bed. Put another way, the fact of marriage does not automatically sanctify anything that might go on in a marriage bed. The limits of propriety are set by Scripture, and *not* by the consent of the parties. Anal intercourse is wrong whether or not the couple are married, and whether or not they both agree to it. Oral sex in which the woman swallows her husband's semen falls in the same category. Her anus is not her vagina and neither is her mouth.

Of course, men who are trained by professional lusters can have a problem with this type of argumentation. They might argue that the Bible doesn't explicitly *prohibit* such things, and they might point to the passages treated elsewhere in this book which indicate the propriety of a certain kind of oral sex. So how can we make a sweeping statement which excludes such practices? There are two arguments against this kind of thing.

First, this discussion is occuring under the heading of *civilized* sex. Men and women are not brute beasts, and they are not to descend to this level of sexual blindness. Godly passion is not degrading, but there is a type of bestial passion which is degrading. Those who would want to defend practices of this kind are utterly unable to show how they are obeying Paul's injunction to put a distance between what they do and what unbelievers in the grip of passionate lust would do. If they would not draw a line here, where could they draw a line? Christian lovemaking is to be distinct from ungodly lovemaking. Those who want to bring such practices into the marriage bed need to explain what they think that difference might be. Given the kind of lust which drives this kind of desire, they cannot accept that explanation.

Secondly, the Bible teaches us that certain sexual lessons are an aspect of natural revelation. In his discussion of homosexuality, Paul mentions that certain men, "leaving the natural use of the woman," have turned aside to perversion. We have dealt with the perversion in an earlier chapter; here we should note that Paul says in passing that the woman has a "*natural* use." What use is that? Clearly, the answer is what would be described as normal sexual intercourse. It follows that to depart from this natural use is to pursue an unnatural use. The indications of oral foreplay found in the Song of Solomon are in no way offered as a substitite for normal intercourse, but rather are preliminary to it.

While his understanding of the reproductive habits of the weasel were somewhat deficient, the writer of the ancient Epistle of Barnabas still had something to contribute to our discussion: "But also he hated the weasel [see Lev. 11:29], fittingly. Do not, he is saying, be such a person. We hear of such men, who perform a lawless deed uncleanly with the mouth. Neither associate with those unclean women who perform the lawless deed with the mouth." The reasoning is simple. Nature itself teaches us what is a sexual organ and what is not. A woman's mouth is not fundamentally different than another man's, and it is not the organ for receiving seed. Passionate foreplay may be, and frequently should be, very intense. But it should end with the man inside his woman, naturally.

As he grows in grace and treats his wife the way a Christian man should, a husband will recognize that women have their own lessons to learn. They need to grow in grace as well. It is not as though the feminine perspective on domestic affairs is automatically right. And further, it is not as though the woman's view on lovemaking is the standard. Both men and women must learn sexual discipline, with a much greater pleasure awaiting them both if they do. If a man has undertaken his responsibilities as he should, and he has learned what he needs to learn, then he should resolve to lead his wife in the areas where she may need to learn to grow. After many years of a marriage with a ho-hum sexual relationship, a man should begin by assuming responsibility. The relationship is the way it is because of what *he* has done or not done. The second thing he must do is learn himself. He cannot teach what he does not know.

Third, he should sit down with her and tell her what he has in mind, confess his sins and abdication, tell her his temptations, and so forth. He may want to give her this book to read, and ask her to discuss it with him afterwards. He must of course be patient—he will not fix in one night the habit patterns of ten years. As he learns to assume responsibility, the following are some areas where he might have to lead her.

In order to satisfy a man, a woman should be mentally and emotionally prepared for frequent lovemaking. Of course it should go without saying that he should not sexually ambush her all the time, but it should *also* go without saying that he will be initiating frequently. Many women do not really understand the *nature* of a man's sexual desire and how easy it would be for her to quench most of the forest fire. They should try to imagine their situation in terms of a man trying to comprehend what it is to give birth. The point here is obviously not a comparison of the pain involved. The two things are (I assume) not comparable except in this one respect—they represent *alien* experiences to each sex. One of the best expressions of the intensity of this desire I have heard was in the popular song some years back about some men at sea on a shakedown cruise—"you boys want some sex? You can squeeze the sails, you can lick the decks." When men are in the hold of this kind of desire, and there is no lawful way to satisfy the desire, the situation is simply difficult. But when a man is *married* and he can't get satisfaction, the difficulty is compounded with sexual bewilderment. A woman who has learned this knows how to be prepared to be responsive, and occasionally to take the initiative. She needs to be available to her husband, and he should know it.

In order to satisfy a man, a woman must take care *not* to take short cuts. One of the easier pitfalls here is that of being sexually low class. There are certain ways to get short term excitement in the bedroom, but they are thoroughly destructive in the long run. In other words, if "excitement" is brought into the marriage bed by means of pornography, dildoes, vibrators, handcuffs, saran wrap, hooker costumes, whipped cream, S & M paraphenalia, and other leather weirdness, then the end of true sexual satisfaction is already in sight.

The first and most obvious problem with this kind of foolishness is the law of diminishing returns. As this pattern of cheap excitements takes over, the weirdness wears off quickly, and some new and stranger kinky thing has to be tried to get the same effect. And so life grows increasingly bizarre at that quiet suburban house on Poplar Street as Mr. Smith, the yearning and lustful prince, rides his horse up the stairs to rescue Mrs. Smith, the horny maiden in the attic. Somebody needs some wise pastoral care. A husband and wife who know how to occupy themselves with naked wisdom are in far better shape than a couple who need a closet full of accoutrements.

The second problem here is less obvious, but just as serious. When a woman seeks sexual attention from her husband by getting down and dirty, she is teaching him more than the fact that she can provide him with a good time. There are *connotations* to this good time which she almost certainly does not understand. A woman who entices her husband to treat her like a hooker in the bedroom must not be surprised when he carries the lesson outside the bedroom. Men have been sleeping with whores for millennia, and they know what they think of them— which is not much.

A related problem, and relatively common with some young Christian women (who are single and *very* naive), is that of assuming that *men* are the ones who have a problem with various sexual temptations, but that they, being women and all, are somehow bulletproof. They can look at all kinds of stuff with impunity, or so the theory goes. A lingerie shower for one of their number is coming up, and so off they go to giggle over things they shouldn't. "What's the harm?" The harm is that men are not faithful to hookers.

Why should a Christian woman want to look like one? Why on earth would she want to resemble the kind of woman who is easy to use and easier to leave?

It is easy to get men to lust after women they do not respect. And it is easy to get men to respect women they do not desire. The hard part, the part requiring sexual discipline, is learning how to respect a woman as a genuine lady, a class act, and yet, after thirty years, to want to lay her down even more than he did the first time. *That* is hard to do, and it cannot be accomplished if the woman keeps dressing up like a sexual clown.

But there is an opposite problem. In order to satisfy a man, a woman must *study* him. In this respect, there are numerous Christian women who come to marriage with a great deal of naivete, and although they have been having sex with a man for some years now, their condition of naivete has not really changed. This woman has not studied her husband and his desires.

This is an area which appears very different than the previous problem, but at root it is really the same problem. The problem is one of mental laziness. With the previous problem, women can just assume that what the sex toy shop sold them was what their husband would like. But he is a Christian man, and although a whore could give him some short-term fun, that is not the kind of woman he wants to live with.

On the other hand, a practical woman, one who interrupts her husband's amorous whispering with a question about whether he put the garbage out, is not interested in her husband's desires or questions either. A Christian wife needs to learn how to be hard-headed about such things. She needs to think about her husband's thoughts and learn to talk with him about them *without taking offense*. The outside world does have some collective sexual knowledge, most of which is corrupt and a good deal of which intrudes upon our lives. The chances are good that the average husband has picked up quite a bit of information over the years, a good deal of which he may feel he cannot discuss with a prim and proper wife. If she is *really* prim and proper, she might even take offense that he even knows about certain things—"where did you read about *that*?"—and so he clams up and entertains himself by taking his thoughts elsewhere. To take a prime example, that of our president's fornicating statesmanship with his fellatrix, after a year in the headlines, how many Christian couples even *talked* about it? The point is not (obviously) to imitate; the point is to have the kind of communication where a husband is not left alone with his thoughts.

The point in this book has not been to talk about sex unnecessarily. The Bible addresses this, and so must we. Because we as Christians have not gone to the Bible for our answers, we have found ourselves in the midst of a pagan culture which does not hesitate in its attempts to seduce us, and we for some reason have decided amongst ourselves to never talk about what they are doing to us. This, as the consequences show, is a recipe for disaster.

Many men have consoled themselves in their sexual guilt by saying, "My wife doesn't understand my temptations. If she only knew . . ." This sort of self-pity is a poor substitute for a godly marriage and should be answered in two ways. First, if she doesn't understand, the reason is that she has not been taught by her husband. The responsibility for her "ignorance" is not hers. Secondly, the husband who says this conveniently overlooks the fact that he doesn't understand *her* temptations whenever he uses pornography in some way. A wife is, and ought to be, threatened by it. Sometimes the man wants to say, "It's just a magazine . . . what's the big deal?" This applies also to all his other sexual stumblings. In other words, he doesn't understand what that does to his wife. He is responsible to learn. Guilt is a drag. Confess the sin, and learn to walk away. Consider and study what the Bible teaches on this subject. Study it together with your wife. *And live free.*

If a husband is the kind of man the Scripture calls him

to be, if he leads his wife in her vocational calling as wife and mother, if they talk through their various temptations as good friends, if they are equally committed to the authority of Scripture over their household—bedroom included—their sexual life together will be greatly blessed. As they grow closer together, the goodness of God will be evident in their delight in one another. They will be so blessed that they will come to the point where their only sexual frustration is their inability to tell anyone else about what a good time they are having. Which would be a nice problem for them both to have.

"I am come into my garden, my sister, my spouse: I have gathered my myrrh with my spice; I have eaten my honeycomb with my honey; I have drunk my wine with my milk: eat, O friends; drink, yea, drink abundantly, O beloved." *(Song 5:1)*

APPENDIX A

Q & A

I'm a pastor who has a problem with porn. Must I resign the ministry?

That depends on the magnitude of the problem. If you have a standing and compulsive problem with porn, you must resign from the ministry yesterday. The Bible sets high standards in its qualifications for the ministry (Tit. 1:5–9; 1 Tim. 3:1–7; 1 Pet. 5:2–4). If you are not above reproach, blameless, etc. you must step down. The ministry is not your "job," and so the issue is not really what you will do to provide for your family. The issue is whether or not you meet the scriptural qualifications for that office. If you do not, then you should step down. This remains true even if you think the problem was solved yesterday. If you exhibited a long-standing contempt for your office through your use of porn, then you need to resign.

If, however, you have the kind of problem with porn that simply serves to remind you of your lusts and weaknesses, then you do not have to step down. For example, suppose you watched a movie that had some nudity in it, and it bothered you sexually and bothered your conscience. Confess the sin, and learn from it. This sort of thing simply tells you that you are in a battle, and does not disqualify you—just make sure you are not *losing* the battle. In any case, your wife should know of your temptations, and if the problem threatens to grow into something that could jeopardize your ministry, then you should have some sort of accountability with your elders.

From the answer to your last question, it is clear I must step down from the ministry. How long is the restoration process before I can resume the ministry? Or am I permanently disqualified?

The answer here is that it should not really be up to you. Modern ministers too often assume that the ministry is a job to which their graduate school training entitles them, and that if any disqualifications are acknowledged at all, they must be considered temporary. But a man who steps down from the ministry because of moral disqualification should assume that he has stepped down for good. Of course, under certain circumstances, it might be plain to others in the church that restoration is in order. This is because the biblical criterion involved in this is Paul's requirement that an elder be "above reproach." This is not a fixed, static thing, but will vary according to the gravity of the sin, the public profile of the ministry, and the time elapsed since repentance. Given this, I believe wisdom would dictate that restoration to office not even be considered for decades. This means that a man who steps down because he is morally disqualified should make other vocational plans and preparations.

At the same time, it is important to distinguish between stepping down and a sabbatical. Suppose a pastor saw himself as beginning to "lose it," and he asked his elders for a sabbatical in order to be able to concentrate on his marriage. In such a case, he would be able to resume the ministry when the problem was addressed and the sabbatical over. But this is a matter of heading off potential disqualification, as opposed to the first scenario, which was actual disqualification.

I suspect my teenage son might be involved in private sexual sin—using porn, masturbating, etc. How can I confront/help him on this awkward issue?

While this is not always the case, teenage sons are usually more willing to receive sexual instruction from their fathers than fathers are willing to give it. Often the awkwardness of such situations is the result of ignorance, and the ignorance is the result of not talking about it. The place to begin is for the father to study the issue thoroughly so that he has something of value to offer his son. Once this is done, he should simply take the plunge, and say, "Son, let's talk about pornography."

How much skin is too much in a movie?

Christians should have no tolerance for immorality and nudity in their entertainment. This standard can be maintained by refusing to watch movies which have such things in them, or through an adroit use of the remote control. In either case, it is necessary to avoid electronic voyeurism.

I am a pastor, and recently in counselling, a man confessed to me, under great conviction of sin, to having molested some of his foster children. What should I do? On the one hand, he has broken the law. On the other, counselling is confidential.

Actually, counselling is *not* confidential, at least not in this sense. Biblical counselling in the context of the church could always (conceivably) lead to very public church discipline. This is why a pastor should never promise absolute confidentiality. He should always (of course) be discrete, but there will be times when he has a moral obligation to inform the elders of his church, or in drastic circumstances, the civil magistrate. If a man has molested children who are in his home, then those children must be protected from him. Unfortunately, we live in a time when the social workers who rescue the children might treat them as unbiblically as their foster father did. This adds to the weight of the man's sin—he has left them horribly unprotected.

But there is a sense in which there is a biblical

confidentiality. The decision to inform the civil magistrate is a decision which is made by the church and not by the magistrate. A worthy pastor would defy any subpoena which tried to force information from him. But if the situation warranted it, the subpoena would have been unnecessary because he would have already presented the information.

I am a pastor and am concerned about issues of reputation. Many pastors in the public eye have disgraced themselves and their office through various forms of sexual immorality. This in turn lends credence to false charges which are increasingly common—and in a litigious society this is no laughing matter. How should a pastor protect himself?

Some pastors compromise their office through sexual sin—they open themselves up to the charge of hypocrisy. But other pastors compromise the office through lack of wisdom—they open themselves up to slander.

I would recommend that a pastor who counsels should have a window in the door of his office and only counsel women when there are others around. A pastor should not give a teenage girl a ride home after the youth group Bible study. He should cultivate the capacity to counsel women on intimate matters in a way that is warm, friendly, and distant. He should cultivate a passionate relationship with his wife, and their closeness to one another should be *common knowledge*.

I live near the coast and enjoy going to the beach. However, the fashion in bikinis nowadays does not leave much to the imagination. Does this mean I can never go to the beach?

That's what it might mean. If a man can't go to the beach without sinning, then he should quit going to the beach. But if he has the self-discipline to spend a lot of time looking at the clouds, or gazing out to sea like the ancient mariner, then he can do that. A lot depends on the situation, but the principle should be plain. If the situation is a bad business, don't go into it.

Must my wife have sex with me whenever I want it?
Don't be a fathead.

It was a serious question.
Yes, she must have sex whenever you want it. And you must refrain whenever she wants to refrain. You have authority over her body, but never forget that she also has authority over your body.

My wife just had a baby, and thus, according to the doctor, we cannot have sexual relations for six weeks. What do we do?
Two suggestions. Paul refers to the practice of voluntary sexual fasting (1 Cor. 7:5), and such circumstances may provide a convenient time for learning how to do this. At the same time, Paul recognizes in the same verse that this should not be done for too long because a lack of self-control will lead to various temptations to immorality. When that is the case (as it usually is) and intercourse is still not an option, the couple should plan on a session of creative petting to climax.

I am sixteen years old. I know premarital sex is wrong, but how far can I go? Is oral sex before marriage wrong? Is petting? French kissing?
All the things you mention are only biblically legitimate as foreplay in the context of a lawful sexual relationship, which is to say, marriage. Put bluntly, if you are not going to cook the roast, don't preheat the oven.

But the question also reveals that you are thinking about sexual behavior between a young unmarried couple without any reference to the young woman's parents. The Bible teaches a great deal about this, and so I would refer you to my book on biblical courtship entitled *Her Hand in Marriage*.

*I was converted out of homosexuality, and though I know
homosexual sex is sinful, nevertheless, it is a horrible temptation. How can I be free from the ever present temptation?*
The Bible never promises us complete freedom from
all temptations. But we are told to pray that God not lead
us into temptation (Mt. 6:13). Praying this way will certainly help you. We are also promised a way of escape from
temptation when it occurs (1 Cor. 10:13). Studying the
way of escape will mean studying many of the biblical passages on lust (in all its forms), which were cited throughout this book.

An essential part of learning to resist temptation is to
resort to the various means of grace that God has established for all believers, and not just believers who are
fighting homosexual temptations. These would include
membership in a biblical church, accountability to the
elders there for your behavior, hearing the Word preached,
approaching the Lord's Table regularly, and then, in *that*
context, studying and applying what the Bible teaches on
homosexuality.

*A few years after marrying my wife, I was diagnosed
with AIDS. I must have contracted it during my pre-conver-
sion promiscuous years. Does this mean I must abstain from
sex with my wife for my lifetime? Doesn't my wife have an
obligation to satisfy me sexually, since her body is not her
own?*
First, the principle. What we have here are conflicting
obligations. She does have an obligation to satisfy you sexually, but you have a *greater* obligation to protect and nour-
ish her. If you cannot have relations with her without
endangering her, then you should not have relations. I am
afraid I have no sympathy for a man who believes his sexual
needs are comparable to his duty to protect his wife. This
principle applies to all manner of sexually transmitted diseases.

Having said this, a few things should be said about

AIDS. If by AIDS you mean that the HIV virus is present in your body, then I would refer you to the book *Inventing the AIDS Virus* by Peter Duesberg. It is quite possible that your situation does not warrant abstention from sex at all— but only because the HIV virus is harmless.

My wife and I are considering having her breasts enlarged. Is this lawful?

The question has to be answered two ways, with two different motives considered. We must be careful because the principle clearly applies beyond the breasts. Is any kind of plastic surgery lawful? Are braces on your teenagers' teeth lawful? Is make-up lawful?

So the answer is that it depends. If your wife is a normal woman, and the reason you are considering this is that you are both making destructive comparisons between her breasts and those of some centerfold, then your problem is small minds and not small breasts. Your problem is *discontent*. God tells us to be content with what we have (Heb. 13:5), immediately following the charge to keep the marriage bed undefiled. Sexual discontent is a destroyer.

But another biblical principle is involved. God has given us the authority to exercise dominion in the world, and this includes medicine and reconstructive surgery. No one would say it is unlawful to set a broken bone, or for a plastic surgeon to rebuild someone's face after a car accident, or to enlarge a woman's breasts if the situation called for it. For example, a woman might be helped by implants after cancer surgery. Or, if she was *extremely* flat-chested, amounting to a physical deformity, and she sought help from a surgeon, I cannot see how we could condemn it without also condemning braces for the teeth.

So if your decision is being driven at all by discontent, then do not do it.

A colleague at the office is pretty persistent in coming on to me. I confess that initially I was probably too free in my conversation with her. However, I have since told her I am loyal to my wife and am not interested. This has not discouraged her but rather only seems to have fanned her desire. She's pretty aggressive—how do I deal with her?

The first thing to realize is that you have a Potiphar's wife situation, which means that you have to prepare to protect your household before you shut her down. We live in a time when false accusations, particularly of a sexual nature, are too readily received. This means that you must first tell your wife about the situation (which you should have already done). Secondly, you must research the formal policy that your company has on the problem. If it does not contradict any biblical principle, then you should take care to follow that policy to the letter. Third, the biblical principle that you should make sure of is that every fact is being confirmed by the mouth of two or three witnesses. And fourth, you talk to the woman and let her know that the relationship is not a possibility and that there is complete accountability for you in every aspect of the situation.

My wife isn't active in our conjugal relations. She generally does not refuse me, but neither does seem to participate actively and with a will. I am genuinely trying to meet her needs sexually, but she doesn't seem to want to warm up. What's the problem? How can I lead her in this area?

The problem is probably not sex, but rather your leadership in other areas. To address that, I would encourage you to study the broader subject of marriage, and not the narrow one of the marriage bed. A good place to begin would be *Reforming Marriage* and *The Federal Husband*.

But if you have a good relationship elsewhere, and the only significant problem you have is in your lovemaking, then you must make a point of teaching and leading her *outside an immediate sexual context*. Do not try to lead and teach her as though the teaching were foreplay. Talk with her in a non-sexual setting. Ask what her perspective is, and then do some Bible study together on the subject.

If a wife knows her husband has an ongoing problem with porn, and he refuses to get help, should she go to the elders of the church?
Yes, and for two reasons. The first is that even though the husband is the head of the home, no human government is absolute. The covenant of faithfulness which the husband embraced at their wedding was a public covenant witnessed by the church, and if he is being unfaithful to it, then that is a matter for the church also. When the elders address a married man with a porn problem, they are not overstepping their authority. When they do so because the man's wife informed them of the problem, they are not subsidizing rebellion on her part because in this she is *not* being rebellious.
Secondly, in sexual matters, Paul teaches explicitly that a wife *has authority* over her husband's body. When he turns away from her to porn, he is disobeying her. She has every right to bring this disobedience to the attention of the elders.

I've had a long problem with porn. Do I confess it to my wife?
Yes. As mentioned above, she has authority over you in this area. Your problem with porn is as much her business as it is yours. Further, she was given to you by God to be a protection against immorality. This is not going to happen unless you are able to talk about it with her.

Is it best to get rid of the television and VCR if movies are the problem?
A central point of this book is that the problem is not external; it is internal. So movies and such are not the problem. At the same time, one of the important means for mortifying our internal lusts is to flee the external occasions of lust. So, if you cannot resist the temptations created by the technology in your home, you must get rid of that technology. Just be aware that the removal of these

things is not the same thing as removing your lusts. It is a help, not a cure. Men had a problem with lust long before the invention of these things.

How can a single man living alone avoid the temptation to watch porn?

In addition to all the things mentioned in this book, he should seek out situations of informal accountability. For example, he could get a roommate. He should not subscribe to cable if cable is a problem. He should structure his time so that he does not spend large amounts of time alone. If none of this helps, he should seek out accountability with his parents or with the elders of his church.

My wife and I like kinky sex. Obviously there is a line where kinky becomes "sin." Where is that line? For example, what about anal sex and sexual aids, like chocolate body paint.

The line is three miles on this side of the word *kinky*. Think about that word for a moment. It means *twisted*. A kink in the garden hose is not what you want when watering the garden. Biblical lovemaking is passionate, but not twisted. It is intense, but not perverted.

Kinky sex delights in violating taboos and consequently displays a mentality which is completely foreign to the Bible. At the end of the road, *everything* is distorted, even to the point of describing chocolate body paint as a "sexual aid." Why not contractor's glue in gallon jugs?

As pointed out earlier, the Song of Solomon extols being drunk with lovemaking. This is scriptural passion and is completely distinct from an infantile fascination with fetishes and fetish-like sex. The Bible teaches and applauds lovemaking for grown-ups.

My experience with porn has left me with a lot of confusing questions. For example, what sort of language may a husband and wife use in bed? Can obscene language be used in the marriage bed?

Always be leery of those things which you learned from porn. If your use of certain words is employed simply because such words are taboo, and you and your wife are *trying* to be "naughty," then there is clearly a problem. If a couple is using such language because they get a kick out of doing something that they *think* is sinful, then they obviously are sinning. Do not slavishly imitate or copy the pattern shown to you in pornography. Pornography is rebellion, and such words are often employed in order to express that rebellion. It is never lawful to use kinky language in order to arouse passion.

But at the same time, the Bible does not contain a list of "bad words." As mentioned earlier in this book, the word obscene means "off-stage." So with regard to the question of "obscene" words considered in themselves, we must remember that the couple *are* "off-stage," and they are there lawfully. So if such words are used simply because they are *descriptive* and there is no connection to a rebellious defiance of taboos, then there is no problem. The lawfulness of words is always a matter of context and meaning.

What about sex during the wife's monthly period?
The Bible prohibits this (Lev. 18:19), but there are also some restrictions connected to the now-fulfilled ceremonial law (Lev. 15:28). While some argue that *all* these menstrual restrictions are part of the ceremonial law, I would want to argue that a couple should refrain from sexual intercourse during the actual time of her period for moral reasons. The prohibition in Lev. 18 is found in the midst of many other moral restrictions of incest and adultery, and I take it as a permanent restriction. The prohibition in Leviticus 15 simply has to do with the woman's ceremonial cleanliness with regard to her preparation for worship in the tabernacle. So I do not believe a couple today is required to refrain from intercourse for a week after her period.

At the same time, a restriction on intercourse during

her period does not necessarily mean a prohibition of all sexual activity, but intercourse should be set aside until her period is over.

Should pornography be a crime?

The standard Christian political opposition to pornography, now gearing up for a cyberbattle, is a case in point. Every Christian knows that pornography is offensive to God, and as good Americans, as soon as we determine that we are against something, we automatically assume that "there oughta be a law." Because of this, we frequently seek to impose God's standards via humanistic means and consequently find ourselves vainly trying to kill sin with Lysol.

Imagine a prosecuting attorney living at the time of Moses. And suppose some hard-core pornographers were brought in to him. According to biblical law, how would they be charged? With a biblical approach, the pornography would not be the crime, it would rather be the evidence of the crime. To illustrate, suppose some young teenagers went on a spree, breaking into shops and stealing things. One of the first things they stole was a videocam, and they were foolish enough to tape all the subsequent proceedings. In such a situation, we would not think to charge them with making movies of a burglary—we would use the footage to establish their guilt in the theft itself.

To continue the illustration, imagine a society in which Christians insisted that we crack down on burglar movies, but resisted any attempts to punish thieves. The situation would be odd, at the very least. Why do we resist punishing what God requires punishment for and insist on punishments found nowhere in Scripture?

The lesson should be applied to pornography. In biblical law, numerous sexual relationships are prohibited, with civil penalties attached. When pornography is made and distributed, it should simply be used as evidence of the adultery or of the sodomy, etc. If the evidence does not demonstrate a crime addressed as a crime in Scripture, then the problem should be addressed through the governments of family or Church, without the threat of civic penalties, or it should be left alone. We do not have the capacity to legislate wisely where God has been silent. The civil governor is God's minister, God's deacon. He is limited in his authority.

Christians must learn to distinguish sins from crimes. If God reveals His will on a matter, disobedience is sin. If God reveals the civil penalty which must be applied, then it is also crime. But without wisdom from Him on the civil penalty to be applied, the civil order must leave enforcement of God's law to the Church, family, or the providence of God. Such distinctions are vital in order to address porn problems on the Net scripturally.

Can a divorced man be an elder?

The Bible describes clearly what an elder is to be like. Among other things, an elder must be "blameless." He must be "temperate" and of "good behavior." He must not be a "covetous" man, or "quarrelsome." He must have a good testimony with those who are outside the Church. The full descriptions of the biblical elder are found in 1 Timothy 3:1–7, Titus 1:5–9, and 1 Peter 5:1–4.

These passages describe required personal attributes and character—they are not a mechanical checklist. Paul and Peter require us to find a certain kind of man. This is important for many reasons, but early among them is that elders are responsible to replenish their own ranks, and in order to find a certain kind of man, it is necessary for the current elders to *be* certain kinds of men. In other words, when the elders of a church are determining whether or not a new candidate is qualified for the office, they must be the type of men who are *mature in judgment*. They are discerning character, not counting rocks.

To take one example from Paul's list: an elder must be a "one-woman man." These cryptic words require a judgment call. Does it mean "no polygamists"? Does it exclude a man who has ever been divorced? A man who has been married and divorced five times? Taking it further, does Paul reject any man who has been with more than one woman sexually at any time, with or without the marital paperwork? And what about a man who has been married more than once because his first wife has passed away? What Paul says is that an elder must be a "one-woman man." Clearly, when we come to apply God's absolute Word in a variable world, the elders must be men of mature biblical judgment, because they are called upon to make such judgments. To sin in making these judgments is a grievous thing.

Two different attitudes interfere with mature judgment in such cases. First is the sloppiness found in liberal and modern evangelical churches: it begins by decrying "legalism" and "perfectionism," and moves on to consider the biblical requirements as nothing more than mere "suggestions," then as a "noble ideal, but impossible to achieve," and then, not surprisingly, disregards them entirely—dismissed from consideration as "unrealistic." Countless churches have fallen from faithfulness to Christ into fuzzy-minded liberalism because they were faithless *first* in how they selected their leaders.

The second attitude is often a reaction to this modernist refusal to take God's Word seriously. In this reaction, the list of attributes ceases to be descriptive of a certain kind of man and hardens into a checklist. And as with all "checklist" approaches to godliness, a clear arbitrariness begins to creep in—no less humanistic, even though it is thought to be "strict" or "conservative." Countless churches have fallen away from faithfulness to Christ into an unbiblical woodenness because they were faithless *first* in how they selected their leaders.

Thus, a man who slept with ten women before his conversion, but was enough of a jerk not to marry any of them, is thought to be qualified for eldership after his conversion, but a man who married one woman and was divorced from her before his conversion is thought to be automatically disqualified. This version of the "one-woman man" may have had any number of mistresses in his past, but no wife. Ironically, this "strict" approach can wind up accepting men who have a glaring character deficiency with regard to women and excluding a man who clearly does not. It is as though the elders insisted that a new elder not be given to much wine, but oceans of beer are okay.

Now obviously the subject of marriage and divorce does relate very clearly to this qualification of the "one-woman man." A man most certainly *can* be excluded by the biblical requirements because of a divorce in his past. But wise elders will not exclude him out of hand; they will reject any attempt to reduce the evaluation of a man's character to a simple three-step process. The desire to have a handy-dandy checklist can easily be reduced to absurdity. An elder must not be given to much wine. Suppose he *used* to have a drinking problem thirty years ago? Now what? Suppose he used to have a drinking problem three weeks ago? The elders must use their heads as they apply God's descriptive standards.

The church cannot have leaders who are "blameless" by nature. By nature we are all objects of wrath. The blamelessness of the elders is by grace, and the task in considering a new elder is to determine whether the work of grace is real, lasting, and deep. This is not done by obtaining lip service to the requirements. ("Do you have any plans at this time to leave your wife?") With regard to this requirement, the fruit of a man's marriage over time must be evaluated. In other words, is he the kind of man who exhibits single-minded devotion to one woman, displaying for the congregation the characteristics of a biblical marriage? If yes, then he is a one-woman man. If no, then he should be excluded from office. If the question cannot be answered because there is not enough history to evaluate, then consideration of the candidate should be postponed.

Men of judicious character are rare, and the nature of such biblical requirements demonstrates how important it is to have them in the leadership of the Church—"But strong meat belongeth to them that are of full age, even those who by reason of use have their senses exercised to discern both good and evil" (Heb. 5:14).

When the elders are examining a candidate, they should be asking whether that candidate meets the biblical description of an elder *now*, and because we cannot see hearts, whether there has been a demonstrated pattern of God's grace at work, over an extended period of time. Apart from God's grace, no one is qualified.

Sexual Glory

Before addressing our subject directly, we must begin with a number of apparently disconnected data.

Throughout his book, the prophet Isaiah described the days of messianic glory in many magnificent ways. In one place, he says, "And the LORD will create upon every dwelling place of mount Zion, and upon her assemblies, a cloud and smoke by day, and the shining of a flaming fire by night: for upon all the glory shall be a defence" (Is. 4:5). In the NKJV, "defence" is rendered as "covering." John Newton rendered this passage wonderfully in his hymn "Glorious Things of Thee Are Spoken": "Round each habitation hov'ring, / See the cloud and fire appear / For a glory and a cov'ring, / Showing that the Lord is near!"

For a glory and a covering. The Shekinah glory that accompanied Israel was a beautiful shelter, a magnificent fortress, a glory and a covering. Given this wonderful image, the apostle Paul makes a profound application:

> For a man indeed ought not to cover his head, forasmuch as he is the image and glory of God: but the woman is the glory of the man. . . . For this cause ought the woman to have power on her head because of the angels. . . . Doth not even nature itself teach you, that, if a man have long hair, it is a shame unto him? But if a woman have long hair, it is a glory to her: for her hair is given her for a covering. (1 Cor. 11:7, 10, 14–15)

As we see, the words glory and covering go very well to-gether indeed. Given the background in Isaiah, this cannot be a coincidence.

Paul teaches that a woman should cover her head with long hair precisely because she is the glory of her hus-band. Her hair is her glory, and in turn she is his glory. Thus, her hair, when a covering, is the glory of her hus-band. This glory is manifested to all, in the presence of angels. Further, her long hair is placed upon her head, not just to show that she is under authority, but also to show that she wields it. Several chapters earlier, Paul has reminded married couples that a wife exercises sexual authority over her husband (1 Cor. 7:4). And the nature of this submis-sion and authority is displayed to the world in a wife's hair.

But we are sophisticated moderns, and this is all too weird. Most Christians today dismiss this passage as "just a cultural thing." And those few Christians who do believe that the passage is binding today, think that it is talking about women of severe countenance dressed in gray with a doily on top of their heads. No one thinks of it in terms of a biblical eroticism.

We can first dismiss the idea that this passage simply reflects first-century mores and nothing else. Paul says that these truths are taught by nature itself, which is quite a different thing than being required by Graeco/Roman cus-toms. The appeal to nature is an appeal to the creation or-der, and not an appeal to time-bound customs. Paul clearly intends this teaching to be normative in the church throughout all generations. He teaches us that this is the way things are in the very nature of the world, and we must learn to conform to it. And if hair is a woman's glory, the question before us should surely not be how short it can be before it stops being a glory. There is a good answer to this question, but why are we asking it?

But of course those who "obey" the passage with all appropriate reactionary glumness are missing the point equally. We are talking about declaring glory and not about being dour.

The marriage relationship is a private sexual relationship, but one publicly recognized and honored (Heb. 13:4). Those things which are public emblems of this relationship should reflect the nature of it accurately, but this is particularly the case with emblems which are given to us in Scripture. Rings are nice (and lawful), but God has assigned another way of making the declaration.

A woman's hair is designed by God to make a statement to the world. When she wears her hair the way she should, it demonstrates her submission and her authority, it shows her gentleness and her power. A godly woman is sweet, gentle, submissive, and terrible as an army with banners. Her glory shows that she is her husband's sexual covering, a formidable defence and wall of protection for him.

Husbands, what is your wife to you? If you have a decent marriage, you could probably answer in greeting card terms: "She is my best friend"; "She is a wonderful mother to my children." But if you have a biblical marriage, the answer should be quite different: "She is my *glory*."

Scripture Index